D0782821

Black
Sheep

Black Sheep

A Blue-Eyed Negro Speaks of
Abandonment, Belonging,
Racism, and Redemption

Ray "BEN" Studevent
Afterword by My Haley, PhD

Health Communications, Inc.
Boca Raton, Florida
www.hcibooks.com

Library of Congress Cataloging-in-Publication Data
is available through the Library of Congress

© 2021 Ray Studevent

ISBN-13: 978-07573-2381-2 (Paperback)
ISBN-10: 07573-2381-2 (Paperback)
ISBN-13: 978-07573-2382-9 (ePub)
ISBN-10: 07573-2382-0 (ePub)

Publisher: Health Communications, Inc.
      1700 NW 2nd Avenue
      Boca Raton, FL 33432-1653

Cover and interior design by Larissa Hise Henoch
Formatting by Lawna Patterson Oldfield

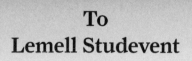

**To
Lemell Studevent**

Contents

1

"Get that blue-eyed devil outa here!"

My angry Southern Black mother, Lemell "Mell" Studevent, was mad—at God, Jesus, and everyone who was ever born since Adam and Eve.

"My heavenly and loving Father, I need to speak with you and your son Jesus immediately," she uttered late one night when she thought I was fast asleep in my bed.

"I'm only asking one favor, please give me the strength of Samson not to kill this little blue-eyed rascal that you've sent into my life."

Momma was beside herself after I was caught throwing eggs at passing cars in our neighborhood. She hated whooping me because she knew I had been through a horrific first few years of my life. When she learned that one of the eggs I lobbed hit a neighbor in the face through the driver's side window, she had no recourse but to grab the thick leather belt she kept for occasions like these.

The thrashing turned my milky white bottom a bright, crimson red, but the pain in my posterior didn't take the starch out of me. I was still hyper and full of mischief, so I secretly placed my sister's reel-to-reel recorder under Momma's bed. I wanted to hear what she was whispering in her nightly prayers. I always felt a special tingle in my wounded soul whenever she mentioned me. Of course, most of the time she was praying for the good Lord to help her maintain her sanity and not kill me for driving up her blood pressure. Black folks seem to have a special relationship between that "last nerve" and high blood pressure. I believe it's caused by the intimate relationship we have with pigs—specifically pork.

When I was sure she was asleep, I snuck into her room, crawled under the bed, and retrieved the recorder. It's a good thing Momma never found out. After all, the conversation she had with the good Lord and his son was private and certainly not for my ears.

That night, I also discovered a piece of my mother's writing:

I once read that blue eyes were a mutation gone bad, and they are better equipped to see in the dark. I don't know if that's true, but a bunch of folks with blue eyes seem to have so much darkness inside of them. The first time I looked into a pair of them steel-cold blue eyes, I nearly peed in my panties. The Klan had strung up my cousin Jesse from a tree, and three hooded Klansmen stared at me. I saw nothing but pure evil.

Sometimes, the evil in the world makes me question the existence of God, but all I gotta do is raise my tired eyes toward that beautiful blue sky above or look at a picture of a royal blue ocean. Growing up in Mississippi, when the teacher asked the class how many of us liked the color blue, nearly all us nappy-headed country girls' hands flew up, including mine. My pencil-thin, ashy arm nearly came right out my shoulder.

When coloring, you had to guard the blue crayon with your life because it would surely disappear the minute you turned your back. My favorite gospel song back in the day was "Feelin' Blue," which our church choir sang every Sunday. We even had our own music, known as the Mississippi blues. Back then, I was too young to know about the blues, but like all us Southern Black folk I would soon learn the true meaning of the word. It kinda bothered me that folks chose my favorite color to describe how they felt.

As I grew older, I wanted to disown blue as my favorite color because I believed that blue-eyed, white-skinned men hated us Negroes with a passion. There was proof all around. Years ago, a White man named John Wilkes Booth murdered Abraham Lincoln, the man who freed us colored folks. In the 1900's, blue-eyed, white-skinned men went crazy. That Hitler fella killed all them Jews and then Lee Harvey Oswald murdered our next Great White Hope, President Kennedy. Then Byron de la Beckwith killed civil rights leader Medgar Evers. Next, and the most painful, was that sinful joker named James Earl Ray who killed the greatest Black man who ever lived, Martin Luther King. It sure does seem to me that blue-eyed, white-skinned men get a whole lotta pleasure killing Black folk.

Now here's a funny thing about Black folks and blue eyes. Every Black family I have ever known has the same painting of a white-skinned, blue-eyed Jesus mounted on a wall in their house. Black folks like to believe that Jesus' picture makes a house feel like a home. God tells us to forgive our enemies, but these crazy blue-eyed men make it really hard for us Black folk to turn the other cheek. I pray on my knees every night for the strength to forgive these evil people.

My grandmother, a former slave, always said that the Lord works in mysterious ways in order to help us overcome our weaknesses. Her words proved to be true when one day, the good Lord saw fit to answer

my prayers by way of a lil' five-year-old, blue-eyed devil he sent to me.
My life was forever changed.

Fast forward forty-five years.

The woman who prayed for the Lord to keep her from killing me
has Alzheimer's. Ironically, I've become the one who feels the need to
converse with God, to plead with him to give Momma her memory
back, at least long enough for her to recognize me when I enter her
room at the Alzheimer's facility. If she doesn't remember me, it will
feel like I've never been born. She was one of the first people to make
me feel like I was worth a darn. If I'm gone from her memory, I'm a
nonentity, a nobody.

I still can't believe that this tough-as-nails, God-fearing woman
has Alzheimer's. She's eighty-seven but has always seemed invincible,
immune to any and all diseases and afflictions known to mankind.
She smoked for nearly fifty years and not once did Mr. Cancer try to
ruin the retirement she earned after working more than four decades
for the government.

Full of self-doubt and denial about what awaits me, I board a plane
in California on a rain-soaked evening to fly across the country to my
hometown of Washington, DC, determined to prove to my siblings
that Momma will tearfully embrace me with her weathered hands the
moment she sees my blue eyes.

As the plane descends over the world's most powerful city, the
white marble monuments shimmer in bright floodlights. I recognize
the once blood-soaked streets, where the divide between the haves
and the have-nots is marked by a bridge or body of water. I locate
the Anacostia River and look southeast. I recall the guys in my old
neighborhood who were murdered there—Junebug, Bo, Ricky, and

Beef—their bodies riddled with bullets. Unlike many of my childhood friends, I was fortunate to escape. The woman I am going to see, Lemell Studevent, was responsible for me making it out of that concrete jungle in one piece.

In the moonlight, I see the Arlington National Cemetery, where her late husband, Calvin, is laid to rest. I think about the lives sacrificed in the name of so-called freedom. It seems to me that when White people think of "freedom," they usually associate it with a famous war or constitutional amendment. When folks from my neck of the woods spoke of freedom, it usually related to slavery or being subjugated by White society.

The man sitting next to me leans over and peers out the window.

"Washington is a wonderful city, isn't it?" he says.

I chuckle a little. "Yeah, I grew up in DC."

"Wow! The city sure is incredible with all its museums and monuments. You mean you *actually* grew up in Washington?"

"No, sir, I grew up in DC. There's a big difference between Washington and DC."

I point out the window and explain why I've corrected him.

"See the bright parts of town? Those are the more affluent parts that are usually well lit and equipped with high-tech security cameras, not to mention all the Starbucks and boutiques. Now that's *Washington.*"

I point south to where hardly any lights are visible.

"See over there? That's DC, an acronym that stands for a number of things: Don't Come, Dead Cops, and Dodge City. Take your pick."

He's not so chatty after that.

Soon, I'm in the driver's seat of my rental car, about to take off for the nursing home. I made sure to get a Cadillac, because Momma taught me to always show up in style. For old-school Black folks, nothing screams "style" more than a Cadillac, and she owned one for as long as I could remember.

Now that I'm entering Chocolate City, I turn the car radio to WHUR, better known as Howard University Radio—Black radio, run by Black folks in the Blackest city in America. I scan the same old mean streets of my hometown. The worn-down buses and scary characters on each street corner remind me of the words of DC native William DeVaughn's famous song, "Be Thankful for What You Got." I remove my eyeglasses because nothing says "come rob me blind" quicker than a pair of sophisticated spectacles or braces on your teeth.

It is so surreal. Here I am, back in DC, but more important, I am *Black* in DC, and I'm on a mission to reconnect and reminisce with my Black momma.

Mell may not recognize the six-foot three-inch tall white Negro she saved when she adopted me nearly fifty years ago. Surely my devilish blue eyes will be a dead giveaway. Even with Alzheimer's, my eyes are bound to extract a gem from her memory bank. Almost from the get-go, she never made much mention of my other physical traits; it was always about my blue eyes. Whenever I misbehaved, she focused more on the color of my eyes than my transgression. She'd gesture with her left hand as the right one rested on her hip.

"Nigger, don't you *ever* think that because you got them blue eyes that you're better than us. Your birth certificate says you *a Negro* and don't you ever forget that!"

Just to spite her, I would instantly begin talking like a plantation slave. "O' course Momma, I be a good nigga'. Toby don't want Massa' to put that whoopin' on my backside!"

I knew that if I was funny enough to make her laugh, I might avoid getting a butt whooping. Momma would try her hardest not to giggle, but sometimes she just had to crack a smile. Better for me if she did. Otherwise, she'd crack the whip on my behind!

For most of my early years, Momma and I shared a unique bond, based on love, race, and triumph. In my eyes, she was special. As a small child, I imagined that heart-shaped blood cells flowed through her veins and eventually ended up in a warm-blooded heart filled with nothing but nurturing love. This was at a time when my biological mother's veins were pumped full of heroin and my father's overflowed with hard liquor.

Outside the facility on Mississippi Avenue, still in the Cadillac, I reflect on the cruel irony that Mississippi was my mother's home state, a place she despised. Will she take her final breath on a street named after a place in the Jim Crow South that caused her so much pain? I want nothing more than for my mother to exit this world with the one thing she didn't have upon her arrival and through much of her early life—dignity.

If she does have Alzheimer's, I know it would devastate her to know that she left this earth in an undignified manner. Her feelings regarding death always centered on her Lord and Savior Jesus Christ. She would often say that God is so organized, even in death.

"Boy, you ever notice how life is a perfect circle like the planet Earth?" she'd say. "It's as if we go full circle from cradle to grave. We arrive as an infant and leave practically the same way as an old person—bald, toothless, unable to walk, wearing diapers, and with absolutely no idea who all these strange folks are, talking to us."

I'm still trying to get my courage up to go inside, I can't help but laugh at the scenario that brought us both here—a Southern Black woman and her white Negro son trying to survive in the Blackest city in America at a time when racial tension was at an all-time high.

Momma and I were a special blend, like salt and pepper. Similar to the subtle spice of ground pepper, she was strong and Black, yet not overbearing. While she may have arrived on this earth as vibrant as a whole black peppercorn, life's trials and tribulations had ground her down to mere flakes. Like salt, my obvious color, I think my presence acted as a binding agent that held our family together in remarkable ways.

Momma emerged from the womb with a reddish hue, no doubt a physical trait passed down from her Indian grandfather, who evidently smoked a peace pipe with her Black grandmother during the Civil War. Unfortunately, that instrument failed to reach the lips of Southern White folks because as soon as she learned to walk, Mell was out in the sweltering Mississippi heat, holding burlap sacks while her siblings stuffed them with freshly picked cotton.

According to the law of the land, slavery had ended long before the 1930s, but you couldn't convince the Wade family of Crystal Springs, Mississippi of such a thing. While Momma was not forced to pick cotton under the threat of a White man's merciless whip, the back-breaking work, done in the blazing hot sun for pitifully low wages, whipped her, nonetheless. She grew up despising White folks, and who could blame her?

It's raining hard. I'll have to make a run for it since I have no umbrella. As I leave the Caddy, with rainwater pouring down my face, I send a prayer up to God.

Please let Momma remember who I am.

I haven't prayed this hard since her husband Calvin, my great-uncle, collapsed in front of me in the sweltering heat of Mississippi.

God didn't answer my prayers then, as Calvin died, leaving Momma to raise her daughters and me, just two years after they adopted me.

With my light complexion and blue eyes, I was White on the outside but Black on the inside—a white Negro in America's Blackest city. Momma hated White people—I was always a reminder of her painful past—and she didn't have to raise me since I wasn't her blood relative. But she did it anyway, even while she was trying to recover from the death of her husband.

While I was growing up, Momma and I were always explaining to others that she was my mother. Things haven't changed much because when I arrive on the fifth floor and ask for her by name, the nurses direct me to the wrong living quarters. After several tries, I finally find her room, but I stop at the restroom so I can muster up the courage to see her. In my head, I can actually hear her telling me to "lift the toilet seat up" as I position myself in front of the stall. Then I hear her reminding me to "put the seat down."

It's almost comical. Here I am, an exhausted, out-of-shape, divorced, middle-aged man with a grownup daughter, nervously washing my hands, tucking in my shirt, and touching up my hair. Will my tinted eyeglasses hide my "devilish blue eyes" that were always a sticking point for her? I want to look confident, but I feel like a scared kid. I take a deep breath and softly knock on the door just like she raised me to do. The quickest way to get your face slapped was to be dumb enough to open a door without knocking first.

"Momma, Momma," I whisper.

The second our eyes meet she pulls her blanket up so she won't expose any part of her body to the strange White intruder.

"Stay right there, mister, and don't shut the door!"

"Momma, it's me."

She reaches into her nightstand. From inside of what appears to be a fake Bible, she pulls out the same gun she used to ward off burglars many times when I was young. Her teeth are clenched and she's got fire in her eyes.

"Whitey, this is Room 357, as in .357 Magnum—especially made for blue-eyed devils like yourself. I ain't afraid to use it. You know why? Because when they ask me what happened, I'll say the left eye blew that way and the right one the other way. I don't trust y'all pale face men, secretly lusting after us sweet brown women. I don't take cream in my coffee! This ain't *The Jeffersons* and I ain't Helen Willis."

I see a faraway look in her eyes as if she's trying to remember something.

"I don't know, there's something different about you. I just saw you out my window. You drive a Cadillac just like Black folks do. Leanin' to the side like you so cool. I even saw you stroll across the lawn, and I said, 'that White man walks like one of us.'"

She exhales deeply and puts her gun away.

"So, what do you want, cracka?"

I feel like I just got gut punched. My sisters were right; the woman who rescued me from foster homes, orphanages, and drug houses has absolutely no idea who I am. I've been reduced to nothing more than a blue-eyed devil, a "cracka" even. Emotions dormant for years rise up to the surface with a vengeance. I have heart palpitations and feel light-headed. Momma has resurrected painful feelings of abandonment I thought I had put to rest after becoming a father to my own child.

I feel naked, ashamed and vulnerable. I am angry with myself for being so selfish, unable to bridle my emotions when I should be focusing on the fact that my mother has succumbed to this horrific and debilitating disease. I am angry because I can't believe that the painful feelings I suffered as a small child have come back, as if I hadn't learned anything. Most of all, I am angry because, up until now, I believed I had come to terms with being abandoned by my biological parents. Evidently, that wound is still wide open.

It dawns on me that I still have one last lesson to learn from my mother. She always said that I could never run from my past and sooner or later we all have to deal with the scars of our childhood. But that's a hard lesson to learn. She is the only person who has given me reason to trust anyone, but instead of feeling gratitude and accepting the truth of what is happening right now, I am ready to unload my anguish on her. I take a deep breath, bite my tongue, and compose myself, but then Momma hits me with a verbal body blow.

"Whitey, why do all honkies always start feeling some sort of pity for colored folks when we are about to die? Is that what you people call "White guilt"? I don't want your pity. Look up on that wall. I dropped out of eighth grade so I could join my siblings picking some hillbilly's cotton down in Mississippi. At the age of sixty-six, I went back to night school to get my college degree. Of course, I went to Howard University because you see that's a Black school, and I was tired of begging White folks for a handout."

What she is really looking at is her GED diploma mounted on the wall. In her broken memory, she thinks she has gone to college. Momma always dreamt of going to Howard University, a historically Black college and university (HBCU) that is one of the premier higher education institutions in the country. There is no way I am going to correct her. She never made it to Howard, but she busted her back to make sure her daughter and granddaughter did.

I gather myself. It doesn't matter how long it will take because I am determined to convince this woman that I am her adopted son. I remove my glasses and move closer so she can get a better look and hopefully recall my face.

"Look, Momma, it's me, Ben. My real name is Ray, but the family nicknamed me Ben, which stands for blue-eyed Negro. Remember? Or maybe you remember me as Scoot."

Scoot had become my lifelong nickname as I got older. Ben was a joke my biological father came up with when I was little.

She squints her eyes, maybe to spark recognition, then suddenly, as if she's seen a ghost, she starts whispering names.

"Dr. King, Lincoln, President Kennedy...all killed by White folks with blue eyes."

Her brown eyes widen and she starts screaming as she pushes an emergency call button. "Nurse! Nurse! Nurse! This White man is trying to kill me! He trying to trick me because they think we are all stupid. That's how they do it before they swing us from a tree!"

I tell the nurses that Momma is my mother.

"Yeah, sure you are," says an old Black nurse, "and I'm Michelle Obama."

Another lighter skinned nurse adds her two cents.

"Oh, you one of them New Orleans Creole niggas? Bright, light, and passing for White?"

I laugh and show them my license with the same last name, but Momma keeps yelling.

"Get that blue-eyed devil outta here!"

They call for backup. More nurses rush in and sedate Momma. They tell me to come back in thirty minutes. I go for a walk and accidentally stumble into the morgue, where the attendant tells me that many residents die with no next of kin, and if no one claims them within thirty days, they are cremated in the basement.

My mother has fewer days in front of her than I would like. I ponder my next move.

"Studevents never quit," Momma often said. She would also point out that our family was bred to be hustlers, so I decide to use her own words against her to convince her that I am her son by telling her our story from the beginning. My idea is to hustle Momma to get her to relax. Prior to my arrival, her doctor had told me that under sedation she would be more likely to listen to me. I ask the nurses to give her something that will put her at ease, and ever the hustler, I borrow a doctor's white lab coat.

I'd also been told that an obscure object can trigger an Alzheimer victim's memory. Since Momma showed that she still is fond of Cadillacs, I dig through her closet and find a box of old family photos, including one of Calvin's first Caddy, a gold 1970 Coupe de Ville.

The sedation is wearing off and Momma is moaning. I dim the lights, so she won't be startled when she opens her eyes. I'm depending on the white lab coat to provide enough cover to keep her calm.

"How am I doing, Doc? Why is it so dark in here?"

Relieved that my disguise has temporarily fooled her, I tell her that getting too much sunlight is not good.

"The sun is only harmful for White folks, not us Black folks," she says.

The first item I show her are my rental car keys and a picture of her by the old Cadillac she used to drive.

"Miss Studevent, do you remember your husband's first Cadillac?"

"It's Mrs., Doc, not Miss."

Knowing that my mother has a propensity to correct people when they don't have their facts straight, I opt to use that as a strategy.

"Mrs. Studevent, please shut your eyes because I'm going to tell you a story. At any time, if you remember anyone or if I misstate any facts, please open your eyes and correct me."

"Could you please step back away from the bed?" she says. "I'm not comfortable having a strange White man standing over me. What if I fall asleep?"

I step back.

"What color are your eyes?"

She can't see the color behind my tinted glasses, so I lie.

"They're brown. You know, my mother taught me to never trust people with blue eyes."

She nods.

"You right about that!"

"Mrs. Studevent, there was once a little White kid named Ray..."

2

"Listen to the pain coming from the soul of a Southern Black woman."

My birth mother, Jackie Rogers-Studevent, was a heroin junkie, with dark hair, tall and extremely thin, like a willow reed. The drugs took their toll on her formerly beautiful appearance. Her once lovely face became sunken and droopy, and her incredibly striking blue eyes were ringed with dark circles.

My birth father, Raymond Studevent Sr., was a Terrance Howard type, and, according to my mother, was incarcerated at the time I was born.

As the offspring of a White mother and a Black father with such a light complexion, I looked White as White could be, with fair skin, wavy hair, and blue eyes, just like Jackie. I showed no physical evidence of being a child of mixed race.

Rumor has it, my father was the first one to call me Ben. Since I don't recall every detail of my childhood, I am relying on Momma and others. Knowing how she felt about White people, especially about a White woman who would allow drugs to come between her and her child, I have to wonder if she may have exaggerated the tales just a bit.

We lived on skid row in a roach-infested apartment building. Although my first few years were spent around drug paraphernalia, such as spoons, foil packets, rubber hoses and lighters, my mother always wanted me within her sight. I think she wanted to protect me from unsavory characters who might have tried to sexually abuse or harm me. After all, she was forced to leave the comforts of home at the impressionable young age of twelve because her sick and demented stepfather kept trying to rape her. Sadly, when my grandmother tried to pull him off my mother, he hit her in the mouth with the butt of a shotgun and knocked out all of her front teeth.

While my mother allowed drugs to come between us, I am grateful that I was never sexually violated. But every family has its secrets and my biological mother's clan was no different. As a child, I heard phrases I didn't fully understand.

"He doesn't look like the rest of his siblings."

I was quite familiar with the inferior feeling of not looking like anyone else in the family. Modern technology has exposed many of these family secrets that were swept under the rug or deeply buried. Nowadays, folks can easily research family records or use DNA tests to determine the identity of their paternal parents.

Lemell always liked to recount the numerous traumatic events that took place during my early years, like the time she and Calvin rescued Jackie as she sat on a curb, holding me in her arms. Apparently, Jackie had barely escaped a burning apartment building, which had been set on fire during the riots following the assassination of Martin Luther King Jr.

Howard University also rang loud and proud in the Studevent household, and no one in the family was a better spokesperson for this historically Black institution of higher learning than Lemell Studevent. "Howard this and Howard that" constantly came out of her mouth. She often subjected us to this repetitive recitation of the proud history of African-American surgeon Charles R. Drew, who pioneered methods of storing blood plasma for transfusions and organized the first large-scale blood bank in the U.S. However, in a cruel twist of irony, the name Howard would come to mean something entirely different in the depths of my consciousness and it tortured me for many years.

I read somewhere that a person tends to bite their bottom lip when recalling traumatic events in their lives. It feels as though I may chew off my entire bottom lip as I tell this story.

When I was four years old, my biological mother gave birth to a baby boy, named Howard. According to family members, the reason she named him that was because he was born at Howard University Hospital. When I was born, it was named Freedman's Hospital because from the time it first opened it was the only place where former slaves could get medical care, hence, "freed men." I was one of the last infants born there before the facility became Howard University Hospital.

Baby Howard became a part of our family for a short while until one day, he was gone, just like that—and under tragic circumstances. Depending on who you speak with, the facts surrounding the case are sketchy and vague. During a big party, my mother got incredibly intoxicated and fell into a blackout stupor in the bed where Howard and I were sleeping. She rolled on top of him and suffocated him to death. My mother's friends fabricated a ridiculous story—that I rolled over on Howard and killed him.

This was preposterous, since I was hardly bigger than he was. Who knows why they said this—probably to hide the fact that there were illegal drugs in the house—but I believed it and the guilt impacted me for years. I couldn't speak up for myself, so I was a convenient scapegoat—collateral damage of a horrific situation.

The police sirens wailed for what seemed like forever, adding to the chaos and fog of the night. I didn't understand that Howard would never come back. I just knew that something awful had happened and that it couldn't be undone.

For months, I lived in an orphanage and sometimes with different relatives while all the legal stuff was unfolding. I don't remember much of that time period.

According to Lemell, the reason everyone said I suffocated Howard was to prevent the authorities from arresting Jackie and taking me away from her, which in retrospect would have been doing me a great favor. Whenever I asked Lemell about the "Howard" story she pretended not to know anything about it. I often overheard on the phone, saying, "No way that boy fell asleep on top of that baby. They all lied. But we know the truth and they know we know it."

It wasn't until I reached my late teens that Lemell finally alleviated my mental anguish by telling me what really happened that night. She wanted me to forget about it and with the passing of time, the horrific experience began to fade. Nevertheless, I still believed that I had taken my little brother's life.

Lemell said that Howard's father was extremely angry at me because they told him I had accidentally killed his son. Of course, it stands to reason that if he had discovered that the person really responsible for suffocating Howard to death was in fact the drunk mother of their child, there's no denying he would have unleashed his wrath on her.

The saving grace for Jackie was that someone on her side was always secretly reporting back to the Black folks. They were afraid to confront her because she wasn't the type who scared easily. If you got caught up in her wrath, she was liable to kill you and not blink. Her rough upbringing left her no other recourse but to be tough in order to survive as a White woman on skid row in the violent, drug infested streets of DC.

Lemell claimed that her husband and my father's uncle, Calvin Studevent, wanted to raise a fuss and take names and kick butt, but she talked him out of it. While he was a gentle giant, the former boxer, Korean War veteran, and Marine Corp Master Sergeant in Calvin would take over when he was provoked, and when that happened, watch out!

Instead, Calvin and Lemell told Jackie they had heard about them blaming me for Howard's death. Calvin said that he would let the matter rest if Jackie allowed him and Lemell to have temporary custody so they could get me out of the orphanage. Otherwise, his "buddies" and former Marine Corp pals in the DC Police Department would put the pressure on everyone at the party that night to come clean about what really happened. That meant Jackie would have gone to prison. Of all the trauma and volatility I witnessed during my early years, the "Howard incident" was the worst. However, despite the egregious nature of that incident, an event that occurred a few months later landed me in the hands of the welfare department.

One day, my mother sat atop a dark stairwell. It was dark and I didn't see her there so I tripped over her and fell down an entire flight of stairs. The fall ripped my mouth wide open, and according to Lemell, I lay on the floor in a pool of blood, and nearly bled to death until my grandmother found me. The scar on my lip is a sobering reminder of my tumultuous childhood.

Doctors said I was a hyper kid due to Jackie's drug use during pregnancy. She swore up and down that she didn't use drugs during that time but the social worker who monitored me because of incidents of negligence didn't believe her. She told my birth mother that one of the side effects of heroin use was how it inhibited the body's ability to produce melanin, meaning it wasn't uncommon for a child to be born with no pigmentation, even if one of the parents happened to be dark skinned.

The social worker noticed that at only five years old I had developed a bad nervous condition of biting my nails. To this day, I have not been able to overcome this nasty habit.

Jackie was oblivious to my needs and incapable of comforting me, as she was trapped by her addiction and a constant need to score. Any maternal instincts she might have had were laid to waste by the drugs. Every time there was a frenetic police raid in the apartment building, which was often, I would run and hide under the bed, inside a secret hole in the mattress, or in a hidden compartment in the closet. I knew that the sound of sirens might result in me going to an orphanage or Mom being arrested—something no little kid should need to think about—ever. I saw lots of things no five-year-old child should see.

While in the hospital, Calvin Studevent and Lemell came to visit me. I had met them several times before on visits to their house. Calvin was a large, jolly Black man with a warm disposition. He breathed heavily because he suffered respiratory complications from exposure to Agent Orange during the Korean and Vietnam Wars. That day, Calvin was dressed in his Marine Corps uniform. I was so excited and wanted to touch all the medals.

Calvin got into an intense conversation with the social worker. Because the courts aim to keep the family unit intact—even if it is a dysfunctional disaster—she told him that I would remain in the custody of the city until either my mother got off drugs or my father was released from prison and was deemed fit as a responsible guardian. Calvin kept pushing, knowing what I would face if I returned to either one of my birth parents. He inquired about taking temporary custody of me, but the social worker said he would need to get the father's consent and pass her department screenings. In fact, my mother's family would have the same opportunity because Jackie had asked her brothers to seek temporary custody.

"Ben," Calvin said, "we're going to get you outta' here buddy."

I learned later that Mell didn't share his enthusiasm. It wasn't just a matter of another mouth to feed; it was the difficult realities of raising a mixed-race child. Apparently, they argued on their way home about getting custody.

"Calvin, are you serious? We have two teenage daughters. How in the world are we supposed to raise a white, blue-eyed Negro in a house full of colored folks on the Blackest side of the Blackest city in America? No White bus drivers, cops, or trash men dare come around because they would get killed. You'd be lucky to even get a taxi to come around there after dark, and you expect this boy to survive in that jungle? Besides, we don't even know what name to call him. Ray, Raymond, Scoot or Scoop. I can't stand his daddy so I ain't calling him Raymond. And *Ben*, psst, no child living in my house is going to be named after some pet rat Michael Jackson is singing about. We'll call him Ray or Scoot."

Calvin reminded Lemell that he was a former light heavyweight boxing champ in the Marines and that he would teach me to defend myself. He had made me a promise, after all, and would do anything to protect me.

He visited my father in jail to convince him to grant him temporary custody of me.

"Fool, you don't deserve that boy and what in the world are you doing messing around with a White girl at that?"

My father was a lean, handsome, light-skinned, fast-talking street hustler whose parents had abandoned him when he was twelve.

"The president talked about integration so, hey, I'm just doing my part. I'm light-skinned for a Black man. I may as well start this race mixing thing so it's not so drastic for White folks," he replied sarcastically to Calvin.

But he signed the consent form, and Calvin asked him one more question before he left.

"If your son's name is Ray why does everyone call him Ben?"

"B-E-N," my father said, spelling out the letters. "Blue...Eyed... Negro."

On the day of my custody hearing, my mother's two uncles, Tommy and Bobby Lee, argued with one another in the courthouse lobby. They lived across the Potomac River in Northern Virginia, where racial tensions ran high.

"Listen Bobby Lee, that boy looks like one of us, but he ain't one of us," Uncle Tommy said. "You know how them colored kids are. They start out real light with curly hair but then by the time that boy is a teenager he got a wide nose, darker skin, and that kinky Afro hair. Folks 'round our parts ain't too fond of them type. They'd rather it be an all-Black baby than some kid from a White girl messin' around with a Black boy. Next thing you know, we got a cross burning in the front yard! You saw what happened when they brought that Coach Boone to coach the Titans. Folks nearly burned the city down. I'm out of this and so are you."

The uncles declined to pursue custody of me, so the judge granted temporary custody to Uncle Calvin and Aunt Mell. Calvin was ecstatic, while Mell—who became Momma—appeared to be upset. She suppressed her trepidation so the judge wouldn't question his decision. Black folks tend to be quite animated, and I found out that right up to the moment they got to the courthouse Mell and her two daughters had laughed and argued with Calvin about bringing "a super-hyper and goofy White boy" home with them.

I'll never forget the ride to my new home. Calvin had parked his big gold Cadillac right in front of the courthouse. It wouldn't have mattered to me if they had picked me up on a bike. All I cared about was that these relatives were taking me to live with them. I'm sure it was weird that this Black family was adopting the only White kid in the place. The older kids, the Black teenagers who had a better understanding of the racial issues in America, likely resented the fact that these Black folks chose to adopt a White kid over one of them.

Even at that young, impressionable age, I knew that I looked different from everyone else. The issues of racial identity and abandonment would later dictate many of the decisions that I would make and lead me into a life of confusion, seclusion, and delusion. While approaching the Cadillac that day, I desperately wanted to trust that these Black folks were genuine and would not abandon me as my biological parents had done.

I have never felt any anger or resentment toward my biological mother because in a strange way I always felt she loved me. I just never felt normal and could never relax. I was desperately hoping that these Black folks would provide me with some stability. I just wanted to relax, but my brain never stopped spinning and I could never focus very well.

By then, I had spent many sad nights in different houses, with strange people, feeling like a lost soul. I also wasn't a stranger to staying overnight at the local hospital as the child of a drug-addicted parent, sleeping in a nurse's station, waiting for "someone" to come pick me up.

After all that, I wanted safety and someone to care for me. I had fractured my skull once from some sort of abuse that no one in the family was willing to discuss. My legs had been burned nearly to the bone when my cousin accidentally spilled a hot chicken potpie on me. Then there are the emotional gashes you can't see. Now, at age fifty-four, I still chew my fingernails to the nub from nerves I have never been able to completely control.

But on that day, my new father, Uncle Calvin, the imposing figure behind the wheel of his 1970 Cadillac Coupe de Ville, became my hero. He's what a father is supposed to be. He always seemed to be in a great mood and my face lit up every time I caught a whiff of his signature Brut 33 cologne. Warm, caring, and just plain decent, I admired him deeply. I watched his every move, modeling how to act, how to be a man.

On the ride home from the orphanage, I sat nestled in the back between two girls who had been my cousins but were now my sisters. Momma sat quietly up front in the copilot position. She fired up a cigarette and handed her lighter to Linda so she could light hers, too. My new older sister was a real sista' in the Blackest sense of the word. Linda was a twenty-year-old student at Howard University, the college you went to if you wanted to discover what it meant to be Black. If you didn't know, Howard would certainly teach you. All you had to do was enroll in this fine institution. I had already liked Linda because during previous visits she sometimes let me light her cigarette and take an occasional puff. I got nervous because she got mad if I wet the filter too much with my lips. Linda always wore shades, which gave her a mysterious aura, like the male version of Linc from *Mod Squad*.

While Calvin looked pretty suave driving a Cadillac, he paled in comparison to the coolness of his oldest daughter. Linda, with her huge Afro and big shades, was a pioneer during the embryonic stages of what we have come to know as the modern day "strong, indepen-dent, Black woman." Her enormous Afro, comparable to that of soul sister number one, Angela Davis, legitimized her Blackness, not just because of its size but because it was impeccably sculpted and main-tained by an authentic "Made in Detroit" red, black, and green pick, emblazoned with a Black Power fist. Linda's Afro was so big she had to get in the car feet first so she could turn around and guide her head into the back seat without disturbing the symmetry of her perfect coif. Maybe I imagined it, but I think I even remember Calvin asking her to move her head to the side so he could see out of his rear-view mir-ror. At that time, the size of one's Afro shouted to the world the depths of one's pride in being Black. It echoed the words of James Brown's Black Power anthem, "Say It Loud—I'm Black and I'm Proud."

Of course, Linda smoked Kool. Before lighting up, she pulled out a mirror and gave her hair a generous blast of Afro Sheen hair spray. I was infatuated with the way it swayed back and forth. Linda began to pack her cigarettes by smacking the end against her hand really hard to push all the tobacco toward the filter. To see a cool, Black woman open up a new pack of cigarettes was theatrical. I was a cap-tive observer watching Linda let the cigarette hang off her bottom lip while she closed the pack. Then she tilted her head back and blew a perfectly round circle of smoke that would have made Pocahontas

and all Native Americans proud. I believe Lemell's father is half Choc-
taw Indian so that might explain it.

Sadly, the first lesson I learned in the car that day was that things
could go from good to bad in a New York minute. Fascinated by
Linda's hair, wondering what it felt like inside that enormous sphere,
I reached over and pushed my hand into it. The way she reacted you
would have thought a meteor had just crashed into us. She abruptly
flicked her cigarette out the window and grabbed my hand so tight
she nearly cut off the circulation.

"White boy, if you want to make it home alive, don't you ever, ever,
EVER touch a Black woman's 'fro!"

I was so startled I nearly started crying. Calvin proved to be my
protector as he set Linda straight for her overreaction. Up to that
point, no one had ever defended me. He was my hero now, for sure.

Cookie, a moody and smart fourteen-year-old, sat on my other
side. Every time I saw her, she had a book in her hand, and this time
in the car was no different. She found the entire Afro-puncturing
episode quite amusing. Cookie was the polar opposite of Linda. She
was a "plain Jane," who hated cigarette smoke with a passion. She was
more of a quiet assassin who could literally annihilate a person with
her words, or a death stare that would send chills up one's spine. She
could destroy you with words partly because people didn't understand half of the words she used. It wasn't long before I totally understood her words, such as "honkey." Cookie wasted no time letting me
know that she didn't have a problem afflicting bodily harm upon my
fragile little White body. I had heard the phrase, "I will punch you
in your face," but Cookie took it a step further by telling me that she
would "punch me *dead* in my face." I was a bit nervous but once again,
my new hero, Calvin, nipped her threats in the bud.

Calvin also showed me that there is an unspoken art to driving a Cadillac. I don't know where Black folks learned this technique, but it signified the essence of what it meant to be cool, the one word that would define everything in my life, starting from the moment I got into the car.

Cadillac driving was a ritual. Calvin would slide his pant leg up so it wouldn't touch the car floor. He would pucker his lips against his teeth, take a quick sniff, straighten the brim of his hat, and then take one last look at himself in the mirror before starting the car. He'd lean slightly toward his door and, using the middle finger of his right hand, pull the gearshift down slowly. I don't think he ever touched the steering wheel with his fingers. His palm controlled it like he was the helmsman of the Titanic. And before he could get into full cool mode, he had to turn on the radio and push in an eight-track tape.

My eyes grew big as we drove through the streets of Chocolate City and entered the side of town known as "Dark Chocolate City." In the early 1970s, DC was about 75 percent Black, but once you crossed the Anacostia River you were in Dark Chocolate territory, the "darkest side" of town, where the population was about 99.9 percent Black. The area I came from was rough but it was close to Capitol Hill and the White House so there was a "White presence" around, which altered how people perceived it.

I used to wonder why my biological mother always took taxis instead of the bus. I figured she wouldn't spend money on a taxi when she could use it to score a fix. Of course, I didn't know the level of her addiction, and truth be told, it was simply far too dangerous for a White woman to ride a city bus alone in the days after the Martin Luther King riots.

As we drove further, the subject of music came up and I heard the word "funky" used to describe the latest sounds, at that time to describe songs from two of the most popular movies in the history of Black cinema: Isaac Hayes's theme from "Shaft" and Curtis Mayfield's title hit "Superfly." They were the funkiest jams of that time and some would even say of all-time.

While these songs were Black Power favorites, Calvin's next move on the car radio nearly caused another riot in the DC streets. During one of his overnight stays with me in the hospital, he heard me singing Tanya Tucker's "Delta Dawn" so he wanted to surprise me with the eight-track so we could sing it together.

His first mistake was ejecting Lemell's favorite tape, Al Green's "Let's Stay Together." The second mistake was rolling the window down. And his biggest mistake was inserting the new tape. Tanya Tucker is a "Black" sounding name, so if Calvin had said, "We are listening to Tanya Tucker," they all would've thought it was a Black woman from somewhere like Detroit. We began to sing the lyrics and before we could finish the first verse, Cookie, Linda, and Lemell started laughing at us before they started spewing insults.

"Daddy, we said funky! Not honky!"

Lemell laughed. "I know you don't think we are riding through the streets of DC. listening to that hillbilly nonsense!" she said.

Calvin turned up the volume, but three voices of disapproval rang out loud and crushed our first moment of bonding. Calvin was nearly thrown out of his own car by those three angry Black females.

Eventually, in 1972, Calvin and I enjoyed our fill of "Delta Dawn" and the better version by Helen Reddy the following year. We also established sort of a family anthem with Sly and the Family Stone's "Family Affair."

No matter how "funkified" Isaac Hayes and Curtis Mayfield sounded, one album during that era captured the plight of life in the Black community. Many would argue that Stevie Wonder's "Living for the City" was the anthem for inner city Black folks and I understand that line of thinking. However, I don't think any Black person from that era would not agree that DC native Marvin Gaye's classic album *What's Going On* was the most powerful, relevant, and most significant album of that time.

Despite being a tad aggressive at first, I liked Cookie and Linda, and they seemed to embrace the idea of having a little brother. They always made me feel loved and understood the madness I had come from. The only problem they had with me was my apparent inability to keep from peeing all over the toilet seat. I sprayed so much urine around they thought I was trying to spell my name, like boys who get quite a thrill from spelling their names in the snow while urinating. The toilet issue would soon be addressed in a major way.

I peeked out the window of the car as we approached the house and saw that the surroundings were rather rugged. My cool new father was a former sergeant in the United States Marines but I had no clue what that meant, except that he could kick butt and handle any threats to his family. Once again, he proved to be the father I so dearly desired when he put the car into park outside my new home and told me to come sit on his lap. I got the thrill of a lifetime when he allowed me to steer the giant land yacht into the driveway. As I stepped out of the Caddy, a police car came around the corner. I took off screaming because I was terrified of the police. To my amazement, the officer got out and shook hands with Calvin. They had served together in the Korean War. Calvin was friends with everyone, even the police. It didn't get any better than that.

More exciting new experiences awaited me inside the house. Lemell bought me a new set of clothes and cool sneakers. Before I could put them on, she escorted me to the bathroom to give me a good washing. As she scrubbed my scrawny, White body raw, she kept muttering.

"Boy, you ain't gonna embarrass me looking all filthy with those hand-me-down cheap rags you wearin!"

I quickly learned the importance of dressing nice and making sure that my appearance reflected well on the Studevent name. Lemell rarely left the house without pulling herself together and wearing something classy. It wouldn't be long before I discovered a whole new level of rules for church attire. Even the poorest families in our community seemed to find the way and means to look good for the Lord.

Lemell took me to the toilet and explained the first rule in a house full of women.

"Put the toilet seat up when you pee and most important, put it back down when you finish."

I never learned much bathroom etiquette because folks in the environment I came from made it seem like it was normal to pee whenever and wherever you were standing. So right on cue, just as Lemell turned to hear Cookie and Linda reinforce her instructions, I started to pee.

Lemell jumped back.

"Boy have you lost your mind!?"

I thought she was upset about the pee splashing everywhere, but she was alarmed that I thought it was acceptable to urinate in her presence. What happened next was a moment that defined much of my troubled childhood. With a look I had never seen on her face, Lemell paused, stopped yelling and whispered, maybe to God, for all I knew.

"Oh my goodness, no wonder the boy can't pee straight. This child hasn't been circumcised."

I had no idea what she was talking about, but it must have been important because she made me pull up my pants and then she hugged me. Because up until that point, hugs had been few and far between in my life, it felt so good to simply be held. I probably thought, *if peeing on the toilet gets me a hug, I will pee all over the kitchen floor if it means getting some affection.*

For the next few days, all I kept hearing about was getting circumcised. While I still had no idea what it meant, I kept hearing that it might be a bit painful. I learned that Lemell was not a woman easily impressed by a doctor simply because he wore a white lab coat.

She needed documentation to have me circumcised but the social workers said it could take a few weeks to complete. After waiting two weeks, she took me to Howard University Hospital, figuring she could convince a reasonable doctor to perform the procedure, but the doctor, who was African, refused because Lemell could not prove she was my guardian.

I had thought Calvin was the toughest human being I knew but I soon discovered that the Black woman from Mississippi, known as Lemell Studevent, was about to dethrone him. She unleashed a barrage of "Black woman attitude" I had never imagined her being capable of delivering. In many African cultures, women are treated as second class citizens who aren't allowed to talk to men in such a strong manner. The African doctor at Howard quickly came to realize that Black women in America don't care if you are the king of the entire continent of Africa. If you got it coming, you will get an earful of "straight-up sister."

According to the stories that make up the Studevent family history, this one is certainly memorable as the first of many episodes when folks did not believe that Lemell was my mother.

In this case, Lemell wasted no time in helping the doctor realize that he had gotten off on the wrong foot and that his foot had stepped on the wrong set of toes.

"Lady, I cannot help you," he said, "because you are trying to convince me that this White child is your son. Excuse me, I am going to lunch."

In response to his attempt to rudely dismiss her, Lemell began to unload.

"First of all Mister! And yeah, I just called you Mister, first, because you addressed me as 'lady.' My name is Mrs. Studevent, not 'lady.' Secondly, I will decide if and when I will address you as 'doctor' because so far you ain't earned that with me. You got that Mr. Negro? Be glad I ain't called you a nigga, but if you don't act right, I'm going to call you that word and a whole lot more. Listen, whatever your crazy name is that I can't pronounce, that white robe and accent doesn't make you White. You ain't special, I don't care if you African, West Indian, Caribbean, Jamaican... nigga, please! Yup, I called you a nigga because you got my blood pressure up. Actin' like y'all better than us American Black folks. You think you gonna come over here and disrespect me? Ignore me? On the land that was built on the sliced and whipped backs of my folks? Remember, you working at Howard, not Harvard, so the White folks got you right up in here with 'Who? Yeah, us Negroes!' This little white Negro with me will be the closest thing to a White patient you will ever see up here. Just 'cause you came over here on a plane and not a slave ship doesn't mean you ain't one of us. So, don't make me get 'niggafied' up in here.

Them little African girls or wherever you from, might be impressed but remember these words about American Black women. 'We don't care how much you know, until we know how much you care. Now Black Indian, put that in your peace pipe and smoke it!'"

She grabbed my hand and we walked out. Just as we were about to exit the building, the doctor called us back and apologized. Lemell apologized as well and admitted that she was under a lot of stress and it all worked out, circumcision and all.

From that day forward, after seeing that side of Lemell Studevent, you had better believe I learned to pee as straight as an arrow.

As I finished retelling the story to Momma in her nursing home room, I felt certain that I had fooled that wicked Alzheimer's. Surely she would remember something of those early days, but she didn't. Instead, she opened her eyes and spoke to me like a total stranger.

"White boy, you ought to be in Hollywood, telling that story."

I pulled out my secret weapon—pictures of her surrounded by family and Calvin's Cadillac, but she had absolutely no recollection of anyone or any car. She thought Calvin was handsome but swore up and down that she'd never seen him.

"There is no way on God's green earth that I would have raised somebody's unwanted blue-eyed White child. I left that mess back in Mississippi where they had us down there working like we was all Mammy from *Gone with the Wind*. I don't wear no do-rag, ain't babysitting no White kids, and, sweetheart, I surely ain't cookin' no pancakes for nobody. I ain't *The Help*."

I felt heartbroken in that moment, but also excited that she could recall her upbringing.

"Okay, so you do recall Mississippi?"

Momma could only remember the prejudice and mistreatment of her family by White people. When I asked her about family pictures, she said they had been stolen by the Klan.

"How can that be?" I said. "You've always lived in DC where the population in your neighborhood is 100 percent Black."

It soon became apparent that her medication had worn off and she was back in her angry Black woman mode. She began to ridicule me. Then the moment turned sad when she began to confuse people, like Oprah and Obama.

"Answer me this, son, and I only use the word 'son' because I feel sorry for you. You're standing here before an old Black woman looking like a lost, sad puppy in search of his momma. Tell me, why is it that White people always run to us colored women for advice when they start to feel like helpless, lost souls? It's that Oprah Obama who started all this nonsense. For twenty years, I've watched you crazy White folks run on Michelle Obama's television show and talk about how ya'll hate yourself. Funny thing is, it got to be so many of y'all that she had to hire that bald-headed White man Dr. Phil and then Dr. Oz to help her out! Y'all folks so desperate y'all got the doctor from *The Wizard of Oz* up on the television trying to help y'all out. Is Oprah still married to Harpo?"

I felt sorry for her confusion, like thinking that Oprah is married to Harpo, the character she wedded in *The Color Purple*, but after listening to her tirade, I was also frustrated because I thought she was doing this on purpose as revenge for me being a White man with blue eyes.

Momma began to complain that I was causing her blood pressure to rise, but I ignored her because my own blood pressure was nearing a boiling point. I attempted to defuse the situation by practicing the old therapeutic Anger Management 101 "count to ten" approach, but it didn't work. I was already too worked up dealing with the demons of my emotional damage to be rational and see the situation for what it was.

The combination of my own racial identity crisis combined with the pain of abandonment were proving to be a recipe for an emotional meltdown. I loved this woman with all my heart and appreciated all she had done for me, but I could not deny that she harbored deep resentment toward me, that I was somehow able to prance through life behind the protection afforded to those who were blessed with white skin and a pair of blue eyes. At that moment, my supposed blessing felt more like a curse.

We locked eyes in a staredown as if we were two gunslingers standing outside a saloon in the Wild West. I held my ground—stoic and firm—even though I was on the brink of going ballistic with a verbal assault. Suddenly, I was overcome with a calming sensation and drew solace in the one man who had meant the most to Momma in her life. While her late husband Calvin had been so special, Momma's love and reverence for Jesus Christ could never be surpassed or questioned. Out of sheer desperation, I decided that I would have to rely on a higher power to help resolve this issue or at least bring about a momentary peace.

In the best Southern Baptist voice I could muster, I politely addressed Momma.

"Ma'am, with all due respect, it would appear to me that the only man who can help us resolve this situation is none other than our Lord and Savior Jesus Christ, and I would like for us to bow our heads and ask for his blessing and that of his Father the Almighty God."

"Boy, what do you know about the Lord?" she said. "Well, that's about the best idea you done had all day because the Lord will reveal if you're lying. Do me a favor. Don't take all day. Your kind talks too much. The Lord is busy trying to answer millions of prayers, and you White folks sure do like to tie up *his* prayer lines. Your bratty, snot-nosed White kids are probably at home texting the Lord with the latest smarty pants phone. You don't need no fancy technology to talk to God. The Lord knows what you need, he just wants acknowledgement so, if and when you receive that blessin' you know it's from him. And I can tell if you grew up in my house by your prayers. So, let's hear it."

I didn't dare remind her that I had left the Baptist Church and became one of Jehovah's Witnesses. She would have called down all the angels from heaven to get me out of her room. There she was, telling me to do something I had been asked to do for much of my life. She was in essence asking me to prove my "Blackness."

I had more than fifty years of that nonsense under my belt so I thought it would be easy. Feeling a tad optimistic, I closed my eyes and reached out to slowly grab her hand. Momma pulled it back quickly and slapped my hand so hard that I yelled out "God!"

"Boy, I know you weren't about to use the Lord's precious name in vain!"

"Of course not. My momma taught me better than that."

"Well, she was a smart woman even though she was White."

"I was going to say, gosh darn it!"

Momma found that amusing.

"Yeah that's as White a word as you can find. Now I know you ain't related to me. Don't touch me again, okay? Now try it again."

After bowing our heads, I began to pray.

"Our heavenly Father I'm offering you this prayer…"

Momma abruptly slapped me on the side of my head.

"No, no, no, and NO!" The reason I slapped you is because you're lying to me. No son of mine would ever approach God in such a nonchalant manner. And yes, I said nonchalant. I know your type didn't think I knew such a word, but I told you I graduated from Howard University. Every Black person who ever stepped foot in any church knows that we approach the Almighty with absolute reverence and the utmost respect. Caucasians act like the Lord is some president or somebody you guys are texting or emailing. The good book tells us that he is 'The Lord of Lords, King of all Kings, the Alpha and the Omega.' These crazy college kids nowadays have done turned those words into some silly fraternity as an excuse to get drunk. Now, try it again, and this time, don't be so Caucasian. Reach deep down inside and pull it out of your soul, boy."

Although my ear was ringing from her slap, I felt a tinge of optimism in her having used the word Caucasian and not some derogatory racial slur for White people. When I asked about it, she quipped back true to form,

"Don't get excited, I only said that because we're talking in the presence of the Lord right now. But once this prayer is over, you still Whitey."

I didn't want to ruin the minimal progress I had made, but my confrontational nature emerged again.

"How is it that you have all this animosity toward White people, yet you have that huge picture of a White, blue-eyed Jesus on the wall and the same depiction in your Bible?"

"Jesus was Black, just light-skinned like you claim to be. You know how I know he was a Black man? First, he walked around town with a group of guys known as the Disciples. Ever been to Chicago and seen the Black gang known as The Disciples? How about the fact that Joseph wasn't his real daddy? Now that's something we know for sure is colored folks' stuff. God's word says that *he* had skin the color of bronze and hair like wool. Now you know how us Black folks are always running late? Jesus ain't came back yet, he late, he a Negro! And at a wedding reception that soul brother performed his first miracle by turning water into wine. You learned something today, didn't you? Hang around, boy, and I'll teach you a few more things. Better yet, I'll say stick around rather than hang around. I ain't comfortable using the word 'hang' in the room alone with a blue-eyed fella, makes us darker peeps a bit uneasy."

I was still digesting that when she continued.

"Then the last reason I know that my Lord and Savior was of the Negroid persuasion is found right here in the book of Matthew, Chapter 27. Jesus was tried, convicted, and executed for a crime that he did not commit! Now only Black men get that type of justice. And the word *justice* to Black folks means exactly that: 'just us!' Now any boy who grew up in my house would not have that bewildered look on his face at the notion that Jesus was a brother. See, back then they didn't have DNA testing, because for us that's a code for the jury when we are on trial that stands for Do Not Acquit!"

We both laughed.

"*Psst!*" I said. "Who are you? Johnny Cochran?"

I was tickled pink because she had finally given me a glimpse of the woman I once knew.

Momma pointed out that it was pouring rain to make another Scripturally based observation about race.

"Boy, it's raining hard out there. Don't know about you but I'm waiting to see Noah's Ark go floating by. Now, Jesus may have been

Black, but I can guarantee you that Noah wasn't. There's no way in the world that a boat full of Black folks could have been on the water for forty days and forty nights and not eaten those two chickens. If it had been me inside that wooden boat, I would have prayed, 'Listen Lord, I hope you don't mind if I mix up a bit of cornmeal flour and fry these bad boys up. Then of course there was also two pigs inside the ark. Whoa! A Southern Black woman with two healthy pigs! Ribs, bacon, pork chops, chitlins...we would have had the barbecue smoking up the whole boat. We would have got off that ark a bunch of fat and happy Negroes. I'm sorry, son, you probably don't know anything about chitlins."

Just when I thought Momma was softening up, she quickly reminded me of why she had such a hard edge to her personality. She paused and began to stare at the ceiling. Then she started whispering.

"Forget the Bible, boy, I am going to give you a modern-day history lesson. You know what we folks call "history?" It's "his-story," meaning it's your folks' way of writing the story of our history. Sit down, be quiet, and listen to the pain coming from the soul of a Southern Black woman."

I pulled a chair up and sat as close to her as I could without making her feel uneasy. When Lemell Studevent begins to speak softly, I just know she's about to unload some of her deep-rooted bitterness toward White people, particularly those in the South. In the past, it had always proven to be a somewhat uncomfortable, yet riveting occurrence so I took a deep breath and braced myself in anticipation of what was about to come out of her mouth.

Momma began to mumble.

"Chicago and Mississippi, *hmm*, the so-called Black folks' promised land. Martin Luther King Jr. was our Moses, I suppose. The Lord let the Jews stay enslaved for 400 years and he let us Negroes stay slaves for 400 years as well. The Jews seem to have recovered much better than we did. Maybe that's why they risked their lives as Freedom Riders in the South. Them folks can relate to the Bible and that crazy Hitler fellow with the strange mustache."

At this point, Momma began to fade into an even softer whisper.

"Mamie, Mamie, I feel for you Mamie. You fought for us Mamie. I know your pain Mamie."

I had always taken pride in being well-versed on the history of famous Black folks in America, especially ones who fought during the Civil Rights movement. However, my ignorance was about to surface in an embarrassing manner. While Momma continued to utter the name "Mamie," I knew she couldn't be talking about her own mother because in the South, all the older mothers were traditionally referred to as Big Momma. At first, I was perplexed about who this Mamie could be, but then it finally came to me who Momma could have been referring to. I was sure it had to be none other than Mammy, the role of the maid, portrayed by Hattie McDaniel in *Gone with the Wind*.

For colored folks, this role was a bittersweet one because Hattie was the first Black actor to win an Academy Award. The downside was that she won it depicting the role of an "Aunt Jemima-esque, do-rag wearing, step-and-fetch-it maid." Back in those days, Black folks figured they would take whatever awards they could get from White people.

However, taking into account that Momma had worked as a librarian for decades and was well-versed in Black history, it dawned on me that she could have been chanting about Civil Rights activist Mamie Till, the mother of Emmett Till, who was savagely beaten, murdered, and mutilated in Mississippi in 1955, at the age of fourteen, after being accused of whistling at and flirting with a White female cashier. Mamie had moved from Mississippi to Chicago, where Emmett grew up. Wanting her son Emmett to spend quality time with relatives back in Mississippi, she put him on a train and warned him about the ways of the South. He was not aware that even a sideways glance could get you killed.

Till's death was particularly brutal, even by Southern standards of the time. He was abducted at night by two men at gunpoint from his great-uncles' house and forced to carry a seventy-five pound cotton gin to the bank of the Tallahatchie River. The two men nearly beat him to a pulp until he was on the brink of death. But they were far from being done with him. They shot him in the head and then gouged out one of his eyes for good measure. They finished poor Emmett off by tying him to the cotton gin with barbed wire and hurling his mangled corpse into the river.

After seeing her son's mutilated remains, Mamie decided to have an open casket funeral so that all the world could see what those racist murderers had done to her son. Less than two weeks after the funeral, an all-White jury deliberated for less than an hour before issuing a not guilty verdict. Years later, the woman who had previously accused Emmett of touching her recanted the story and said that he had never done anything to her.

While Momma could recant many horrific stories of her days in the Jim Crowe South, I believe this one cut her particularly deep because Mamie Till was from a small town in Mississippi, not far from Crystal Springs, where Momma was raised. The great migration North from the segregated South offered Southern Black folks hope for a better life—though that hope was never fully realized.

My suspicions were confirmed when Momma opened her eyes, stared down at her hands and started babbling again.

"They tied that boy to a cotton gin. You see these hands, young fella? They put many o' pounds of cotton through that White man's old rusty gin in Mississippi. I knew White folks were the boss but one day I was determined to shove that cotton through it myself. *Shhhh*, that drunk, whiskey sippin' red-faced White man slapped me so hard one time. I was but a young girl, maybe nine or ten years old. One day, I insisted on putting the cotton through the gin myself. But he wouldn't have it and he yelled at me 'Give me that cotton, you sassy little nigger! Why do you have to put it through the thing?' I proudly stuck my flat chest out, let the sun reflect the shine from my half Indian ponytails and said, 'Mr. White Man, I want to put my hard-earned cotton through that Ginny thing because my great-granny told me that the cotton gin was invented by a Black man named Eli Whitney! A Black man! *A Black man!*'"

I nodded and smiled at Momma.

"Next thing I know, *Wham!* 'No dumb nigger could be smart enough for such a thing!' he screamed. That redneck hillbilly slapped me so hard that I hit the ground and I peed straight down my ashy, bony leg. When working them fields, I didn't wear panties because, every once in a while, you got a full-body breeze from the Delta or somewhere off one of them waters sweep right through you and it felt so good. Now I know what you must be thinking. Get your mind out of the gutter. I wore a long dress for sure. My momma didn't want us messing up our good panties working for no White man, better yet we saved them for singing to the Lord at church on every Sunday. Of course, Big Momma had to beg my daddy, Big Poppa, from killing that White man for slapping me down. The worse part is not that I got the pee slapped out of me, but the fact that I got slapped for saying something not even true. Eli Whitney was actually a White man but rumors around the South was that a Black man invented the cotton gin. History speculated later that Eli took the idea from a slave. Whatever the truth was, that White man hit me so hard my momma felt it back at the house."

I knew Momma was becoming overwhelmed with emotion when she sat up and began to stare out the window. In a seemingly cruel irony, she noticed the Mississippi Avenue street sign. Not knowing if it computed in her brain or if she knew the meaning of it, I immediately pulled the curtains shut and an eerie calm seemed to permeate the room.

Momma abruptly left 1930s Mississippi and brought everything current by comparing the previous generations to the present. While it was certainly a serious subject, Momma inexplicably fell into a jovial mood and started laughing.

"Boy, whoever you are, be glad you got that white skin. Don't think because us colored folks can dance, sing, and play sports that it is a life of joy. Every athlete looks in the stands and sees you folks. Run, brother, run, from Jesse Owens to that Jamaican boy Insane Bolt."

She was on a roll, so I didn't dare correct her by telling her that his name was Usain. When her caregiver walked in to check her vitals, Momma began laughing again.

"What's so funny?" I said.

"You're claiming to be my son! I am actually flattered and appreciate it because the laughter is helping to bring my blood pressure down. Y'all lighter folks ain't got no blood pressure issues. Your ancestors fed us slop from a pig and on top of that it's so darn stressful being one of us. If you're half-Negro like you say you is, then let the nurse take your blood pressure."

At this point, I was desperate enough to try anything to get Momma to realize the truth so I agreed to let the caregiver take my blood pressure. I knew that it was generally higher than normal, and after learning of Momma's condition I knew it had spiked. In a desperate attempt to intentionally get a higher reading, I began to think about my childhood trauma to stress myself out. I felt rather ridiculous, but I was so exhausted I didn't care.

"Wow!" the nurse said. "One seventy over one hundred. Scary indeed!"

"Stay away from all that Popeye's chicken, boy," said Momma.

The caregiver told us that Momma was doing fine, which kept her in a cheerful mood. She was on a roll and couldn't stop taking jabs at me. In an attempt to explain my "pursuit of Blackness" she ventured down a new and bumpy road, mocking me with her words.

"Sir, I know. I get it now. You must be married to a Black woman. Ain't no way you can be that cool and be that Black unless you done sipped and dipped in the brown sugar. Go ahead! Admit it! Your wife is a sista'! Of course, ain't no son of mine gonna bring a White woman in my house unless she coming to clean it."

In true Studevent form, not allowing the opportunity to tell a good joke in front of others, Momma couldn't resist poking fun at me.

"Will any of these pills help me get my memory back so this crazy White man can leave me alone? As a matter of fact, give him my blood pressure and glaucoma medication. I hope you know, boy, because of my glaucoma, I am now color blind."

As a fellow Studevent, I couldn't resist the urge to get a joke in on Momma either, especially since she had insulted me quite a bit. I waited until the caregiver left to let my sass out of the bag.

"I didn't know you were color blind."

Momma gave me the evil eye.

"Why would you know? You don't even know me."

I didn't want to risk getting slapped again by this feisty, unpredictable woman, but I poked my bottom lip out and let her have it anyway.

"I would say you are a lot of things but being color blind is definitely not one of them. You see color real clearly."

"Boy are you calling me a racist? If so, I hope you got your underwear on because I will slap the pee out of you the same way your relatives slapped me and my niece Oprah."

True to her nature, she closed out the subject with a simple statement that summed up my point exactly.

"I *am* color blind," she said. "I only see things in black and white."

"Exactly."

From this point on, Momma spoke lower and slower, no doubt from the effects of the medications the caregiver had given her. I knew the day was done once she referred to Oprah as her niece. As she began to drift off, I knew it was time to leave because my patience was wearing thin and my hunger was growing. I thought it best to leave her alone to sleep. I wanted to kiss her on the forehead but decided against it because she might wake up and try to kill me, or worse, have a heart attack and die herself.

I just whispered, "See you tomorrow, Momma."

3

"I suggest you find your real roots, boy."

"Now that I done had some fun with you," said Momma, "it's your turn to entertain me. Go on and tell me what it was like growing up in my house."

"Where should I begin?"

"If you are this so-called adopted White son of mine, where are the pictures or documentation from your childhood?"

Since I knew Momma wouldn't believe me when I told her I had done the research and it could take a while to get a copy of the adoption papers, I pulled up the adoption records on my phone and began reading.

"Momma, listen to why I am unable to provide documentation at this time. 'The District of Columbia requires that an adoptee must first file with the Superior Court, a Petition to Break the Seal of Adoption. The petition must satisfy the court with a legitimate reason as to why they are seeking such documents. The initial process can take up to one year and…'"

Momma didn't like what she was hearing and quickly interrupted.

"One year! Boy, you White folks take forever to do stuff. Shucks, I can find out what slave ship my family came on quicker than that."

"You can't seem to remember anything as it pertains to me, but you're able to recall so much about slavery and racial issues?"

She pointed to a book she was reading.

"*Roots.* I suggest you find your real roots, boy. Your roots are in Europe not Africa."

She didn't seem to care too much about these details, as she had her mind set on enjoying my company. With every bit of progress I made with her, I had to avoid becoming emotional. It was difficult to watch the woman who helped rescue me from ghetto life deteriorating in front of me. I joyfully embraced any bit of hope that she was warming up to her long-lost, blue-eyed son. As I prepared to continue the story, I strained to remember every detail.

Momma rested her head back on her pillow.

"Okay Mr. Studevent, I am going to close my eyes and ask the good Lord to help me remember, and I want you to start by describing my house and its atmosphere. This ought to be good for a few laughs. But remember, if I think you're lying, brace yourself for another pop upside your head."

"Okay, you got a deal. Bow your head and let's do it."

I could describe nearly every detail about her home. If Momma wanted undeniable proof, a few words would set the table in her home and typify my life as a white Negro boy.

"First, with all due respect, the word that describes the house you kept was exactly that: respect. That word ruled every aspect of how people behaved in your house, family member or visitor. You said that respect and love turned a house into a home. Respect was a direct reflection of how the mother and father treated one another. Anyone who failed to demonstrate respect for you and your husband, Calvin was his name, was met with harsh consequences, even for Linda, your oldest daughter, who was already grown up. You made it clear that any act of disrespect would be dealt with swiftly."

I could see she was listening.

"Giving grown people their "propers" with polite usage of words, like "Sir," "Ma'am," "Thank you" and "You're welcome," was a rule that was upheld at all times. Myself, Calvin and your two daughters. Your other daughter is named Cynthia, but we called her Cookie. We were expected to have impeccable manners. No elbows on the table at dinner. No disrespectful placement of your silverware in the sign of a cross. All these rules regulated your 'Black Woman's House!' When adults came for dinner, you had one way to help us understand what was expected of us. Kids are to be seen and not heard. Never, ever, ever interrupt grown folks when they are talking. One rule I never understood was that the living room was off limits. All the furniture was covered in plastic, and it was viewed as a sanctuary. If any of us were caught in there, it meant our behinds would end up on the receiving end of a thick leather belt."

Momma seemed to be paying attention, so I painted her another picture, certain that she would recall this memorable moment in Studevent family history, despite the Alzheimer's.

Like lots of kids, I enjoyed hiding behind doors so I could jump out, and yell, "Boo!" In my case, I had a tremendous fascination with scaring people. Maybe it's because I yearned for positive attention, and a spirited little prank like this wasn't that upsetting for people, considering all the abuse I had taken in my life up to that point.

"Remember, Momma, you used to work at the local public library, stocking books for much of the day. You would always complain about how heavy the World Book Encyclopedias were, the ones that teenagers left for you to return to their shelves. One day, you came home exhausted and I figured you just needed something to wake you up. In order to appear like a ghost, I cut two holes in a white pillowcase for my eyes. As soon as I heard your keys in the lock, I put on my mask, hid behind the kitchen door and waited, careful not to giggle. The minute you dropped your purse, I jumped out from behind the door and screamed, 'BOO!' Before I could see your response, *BAM,* I got whacked in the temple with your umbrella. The blow sent me tumbling across the kitchen floor. Momma, you didn't stop there. You pelted me nonstop on my head. I screamed, 'Momma stop! Stop, you're hurting me!' You finally stopped. I was curled up in a corner in the fetal position, shaking and sobbing. You whispered to me, 'Boy, don't you ever dress like no Klan cracker in this house.' I had no idea who the Ku Klux Klan was and the horrible impact they had made on your life. I lay there stunned, wiping tears from my face, bleeding from my brow. You wiped the blood away and whispered, 'Lord have mercy.'"

I didn't notice if Momma was paying attention because retelling the story was putting me in some kind of memory trance.

"'I wasn't trying to be a graham cracker, Momma,' I said to you between sobs. I couldn't understand why you thought I'd dress up like my favorite snack food and, if I did, why was that such a bad thing? It was a turning point for you as well. Remember you said, 'What did you call me?' Up until that point, I had always called you 'Mrs. Momma.' I just sat quiet for a bit and tucked my head between my legs. 'I called you Momma, but you ain't no different than them other folks because all you do is beat me, too.' You told me to look at you but I refused. 'Why do you say that?' you said. I yelled back at you, 'Because you hate me, the color of my skin, and, most of all, you can't stand the sight of my blue eyes.' I went to bed, shaken by the whole turn of events. In the middle of the night, on my way to the restroom, I heard you praying aloud. You were saying something to the effect of 'This child has been through so much and he was just trying to scare me, and I nearly killed him.' You were asking God to forgive you for what you had done to me. We never spoke of the incident again—and I never looked at graham crackers the same way. That's for sure."

I was hoping this story would ignite some sort of reaction from Momma. I woke her up since she had dozed off and asked her if she recalled that story.

"It's possible that might have happened."

Since that story didn't jog her memory, I figured I'd tell her others until one struck a familiar nerve. After all, I had an endless arsenal of stories. We are talking about a Black woman with a White child in the Blackest city in America. Normally, Momma and I could entertain a party all night long with our endless barrage of stories. But now, with this horrific disease to contend with, it would appear that our glory days were over. I decided to keep talking anyway, telling the most memorable tales from the early years of our journey together.

"Momma, I thought for sure that a story involving the Klan would rile you up and shake you back into reality. Okay then, how about some funny stories that will make you laugh, even if you can't recall them."

She chuckled.

"Start laughing boy, 'cause this entire Hollywood nonsense you're spouting is one big joke. Let me lay my head back and listen to some more Disney tales."

"Momma, let's leave the living room where you nearly killed me and venture over into the kitchen."

As I began to narrate the next story, which was supposed to be funny, it dawned on me that perhaps she didn't find Black folks on food packaging so humorous. In fact, if my memory serves me correctly, she found the images of Uncle Ben on the rice box and Aunt Jemima on the bottle of syrup rather offensive. Momma didn't think these characterizations did anything but reinforce stereotypes. Uncle Ben was an old plantation cook for White folks. Aunt Jemima was the Southern Black maid who reminded Momma of Mammy from *Gone with the Wind*.

One day, I begged Momma to let me go to the corner store by myself. She hesitated because she was afraid of me getting assaulted. She told me to ask someone to help me find the items on the grocery list, but I was determined to get everything myself. Up to this point, my sisters and Momma repeatedly reminded me that I was Black, that my birth certificate identified me that way. They wanted to be certain that I didn't start having any illusions of grandeur that I was White and better than them. So I viewed this as a perfect moment to prove my Blackness. In my opinion, this was one of the funniest stories we had, and I was hopeful that Momma would remember it. Maybe she had suppressed the Mississippi and Klan aspects of her life, so her memory was not jogged by the BOO story.

"Listen carefully, Momma, because this story is a Studevent classic, one we used to tell at family reunions. After always telling me I should never forget that this is a Black house, I decided to convince you that I not only recognized my Blackness; I had embraced it."

Momma said nothing.

"You gave me a list of six things to buy: bread, rice, sugar, eggs, vanilla ice cream, and milk. That set the tone for the rest of my "Black

Power" shopping spree. I passed on the white bread and grabbed the wheat bread instead. I breezed by the white sugar and snatched a bag of brown sugar. I got a carton of chocolate milk and expensive brown rice. No vanilla ice cream for this Negro family; we only eat chocolate from now on. Finally, although I had never seen them before, I chose the brown eggs instead of the white ones. When I got home, you looked at the groceries and the little bit of change I placed in your hand., 'Why didn't you buy what was on the list? This stuff don't cost no ten dollars!' I quickly responded, 'Well, if we're going to be in a Black house, we may as well eat only Black foods.' Momma, you laughed but you were not happy about the price of brown rice. Calvin bailed me out by saying that brown rice was healthier. You didn't hesitate to remind him how much it cost."

Instead of evoking a response from Momma, my legendary Black food story had put her to sleep. I plopped down in the recliner with a grin on my face and a bit of disappointment in my heart. I heard a chuckle from Momma as she seemed to be whispering in her sleep. I eased closer and tried to make out her words. Her laughter got louder, and I strained to hear what she was softly uttering.

"Pumpkin pie, pumpkin pie! Boy, are you crazy?"

I got excited because I thought the story jogged her memory. Again, she began to softly whisper the words, "pumpkin pie" or shall I say it like us good ole' Negroes are supposed to utter it, "punkin'pie.'

Even though she appeared to be sleeping, I began to recount the story until I heard her breathing more heavily. She had fallen into a deep sleep.

One of the nurses slowly opened the door. "Mrs. Studevent, Mrs. Studevent."

I smiled and whispered back, "Ms. Studevent is sleeping,"

"You'd better not let her hear you call her Ms. It's Mrs. If you are her so-called long-lost White son, you should know that."

I smirked and pretended not to hear her snide remark. I was excited that Momma had recalled the pumpkin pie story and too exhausted to delve into a conversation that had taken place hundreds of times during my life.

As the nurse was leaving, I asked her for a pen and paper. While Momma slept, I closed my eyes and tried to recall other memories from my childhood so that when she woke up I could ask her about them. Surely, one of my crazy stories had eluded "Ole' Masa Alzheimer."

After the nurse left, I leaned my head back, closed my tired eyes and let out a long breath. With a smile on my face, I began writing bullet points for each story so I could be prepared when she woke up. Pretty soon, I had made a list of several stories I was ready to tell Momma.

4

"It's like Dark Vader is your Black father and you're the White Luke Skywalker."

Story #1—Betty Cracker Cakes

I love graham crackers. I remember hearing the word "cracker" quite often in the neighborhood but not so much by Momma. One day, she sent me to the store to get some pancake mix.

"Momma, I bought Betty *Cracker* instead of Aunt Jemima."

"It's Betty Crocker, not Cracker," she said, laughing. "But I see you are fitting in quite well in your new neighborhood. Betty's lemon cakes are too good for me to call her that word."

Next, she asked me why I didn't follow her instructions.

"You said Aunt Jemima wasn't nothing but another fat, Black lady cooking for White people, like that other famous fat, Black lady from *Gone in the Wind*. By the tone of your voice, I figured it reminded you of Mississippi."

While Momma found that episode to be rather cute and innocent, my next question ruined any joy in the air. I thought she would be

55

upset because I spent her money on something else, so I ran to my room and brought down the dollar bill I had on my dresser. I gave it to her and told her that it was for the other mix in the bag. She reached inside and pulled out a box of pumpkin pie mix. You would have thought she pulled out a rattlesnake.

"What in the world is this mess?"

Despite my bewilderment at her reaction, I proudly uttered three words that nearly got me killed.

"My White grandmother, she used to make pumpkin pie and I was hoping you could make one with this pumpkin pie mix. They look the same, so I figured they also taste the same."

Judging by the crazed reaction to the three words "white, pumpkin, and pie," you would have thought I said Ku Klux Klan.

"Boy, I don't care if your grandmomma was Sara Lee or Duncan Hines. We don't make pumpkin pie in this house. If you expect to eat sweets in this Black momma's house, you need to learn three new words. Sweet potato pie. I make it so good, honey, it only needs two words: Sweet'tata pie."

My response, while innocent, turned out to be even more insulting.

"Well, you want me to take it back and get a box of sweet potato pie mix?"

Momma laughed.

"Boy, I'm a Southern Black woman and I don't need no batter in a box to make sweet potato pie. It's in our blood. I make it from scratch."

I had no idea what "scratch" meant but I wasn't going to ask another dumb question.

It wasn't just the words coming out of my mouth that she found irritating. What really rubbed Momma the wrong way was the phony and sneaky manner in which I chose to express myself. Although I was only six years old by then, I had discovered that many Black females thought I was an irresistible darling. That's when the inner workings of my conniving little mind began to emerge. Since she seemed to be a bit perturbed that day, I thought I would play the cute little kid with the fake lisp trick. I recall first seeing it executed by the curly-haired, youngest daughter, named Cindy, on *The Brady Bunch.* She had the most adorable lisp, which was endearing to viewers. Well, that nonsense may work on television and with White mothers, but it didn't get me nowhere with Momma.

Not only did she not fall for my fake lisp shenanigans; she informed me that she had observed me use it on unsuspecting neighbors and fellow members of the church choir. She pointed her finger at me quite sternly.

"Listen here, you little blue-eyed joker. That fake tongue in the lips act you're trying to pull ain't cute. You may have fooled Sister Jackson and the sisters in the choir on Sunday with that foolishness, but it doesn't work on me. White mothers might fall for that nonsense, but not Black mothers. Black folks have a special way of correcting children who can't control their mouth. The back of my hand across your mouth will cure that real quick. Don't think because you got them blue eyes and straight hair that you are special. I will whip your White backside so red it will look like two bright country apples."

So much for thinking I was cute. Momma even killed my last-ditch effort for sympathy.

"And please don't try the droopy eyed, sad hound dog look either."

It became apparent that Lemell Studevent was not playing around. She wasn't afraid to let me know who was in total control.

During those early "get-in-where-you-fit-in" years, I started thinking that I needed to act more like Michael Evans, the youngest son on *Good Times*. That little White girl on *The Brady Bunch* is going to get me killed. I needed to be more Black—pitch Black. Michael was known as the Militant Midget because of his affinity to promote Black Power. I didn't know I was too White to pull off that attitude. I figured it would be better to just shut up and simply stay alive.

Story #2—Say Your Prayers

Although I had some rough moments during the early months with the Studevents, I liked my new family and wanted to please them. I'm sure they found my nervous energy rather irritating at times since they were relatively mellow. The household undoubtedly had a calming influence that I desperately needed in my life, but there's no denying that I changed the level of energy.

I was an extremely hyper child with a brain that never seemed to shut off. I suspect this condition was one of the unfortunate side effects of my biological mother's heroin addiction. I couldn't stop talking, even when I wanted to, as if my mouth had a motor I could not control, and like most kids, I hated going to sleep and despised the words "it's bedtime." My inability to fall asleep could probably be attributed to my mother's drug use or as a consequence of the volatility and instability of my first few years of life.

Momma always emphasized the importance of getting sufficient sleep. As I have heard from my sisters over the years, Calvin never stayed up past the eleven o'clock news. Even though I was often still awake at that time, I was too terrified to sneak downstairs and turn on the only television in the house. First, it was too dark, and second, I was scared to watch TV at night because the shows that late were creepy. *Perry Mason* had a frightening theme song; *Creature Features* was about monsters, ghosts and ghouls, and *The Twilight Zone* was just plain weird. The only other show was Johnny Carson and I wasn't about to venture into the abyss of a dark stairway to listen to a bunch of corny old folks.

One way I could fall sleep was listening to the soothing jazz music coming from Linda's room. I heard so much Grover Washington Jr. I had saxophone tunes ringing in my head. Soon enough, I fell asleep to her soft tunes on WHUR, the same Howard University radio station I turned to upon my arrival in DC.

Linda loved listening to what was known as *The Quiet Storm*, which played R & B love songs and soft jazz into the wee hours of the night. Named after the song, "Quiet Storm," by Smokey Robinson, that show became a staple in Black culture around the country and has been credited with increasing the population of the Black community.

On many sleepless occasions, I would knock on Momma's door and ask if I could sleep with her and Calvin. Momma would always oblige but with one condition.

"Did you say your prayers?"

I was not allowed to get into her bed without saying the Lord's blessing. She wanted to hear the prayer she had taught me immediately upon arrival in her house. Every Black child I ever met was taught the same one. It was quick but sufficient for Momma.

> *Now I lay me down to sleep*
> *I pray the Lord my soul to keep,*
> *If I should die before I wake,*
> *I pray the Lord my soul to take.*
> *Amen*

Of course, once I realized how important the Lord and this Jesus fellow were to Momma, I began using it to my advantage. If I knew she would find out about me doing something bad, the closer it was to my birthday or Christmas I always added a few requests filled with childlike adjectives on Momma's behalf.

"Lord, thank you so much for my super-duper, wonderful and cool new Black momma. Please be there for Momma whenever she is tired so she can make us nice dinners, especially on Sundays when she makes soul food with sweet potato pie. Amen!"

Momma was not at all amused with my snow job prayer but she'd take what she could get because at that point in my life she knew I had no reason to believe in any God. There was something extremely comforting about laying being two people who had rescued me. Also, Calvin had a big pot belly and I always liked to rub on it like he was a genie or something.

While prayer was a highly sensitive issue in the Studevent home, whenever the subject of race was injected into the conversation about the Lord, look out. Calvin spent a great deal of time working and while Momma worked as well, we began to spend a lot of time together and I felt myself drawing closer to her. Despite her initial misgivings about me moving in, she slowly embraced me as well as any nurturing mother. She was incredibly generous with a compassionate heart, but she wrestled with her own demons. None were greater than her deeply rooted resentment of White people, which stemmed from the unbearable heat in the cotton fields of segregated Mississippi.

The Bible is full of accounts where Jesus expels demons from possessing people. Even the presence of the Lord and Jesus in prayer was not enough to rid Momma of her feelings toward White folks, particularly the one who gave birth to me.

People often asked Calvin and Mell if my stay with them was permanent, which of course I hoped it would be. Even so, I still wondered about my biological mother and hoped she would get better. I didn't understand why she had problems; I just knew she was indulging in something bad, called "drugs."

As if she knew I had been thinking about her, she called our house one day. Momma's tone when she called me to the phone alerted me to her strong disdain for my mother. In the months to follow, whenever she would call, Momma would pick up the other phone and listen in to make sure that my mother was not speaking ill of her and Calvin. But most of all, she wanted to know if Jackie had any plans of coming to take me back.

Her voice was always harsh and scratchy, often accompanied by a hacking cough. She always promised me that she was going to come and see me when she was no longer sick, a word adults used to explain to children why their parents weren't around. I occasionally asked Calvin and Momma about Jackie coming to see me. Calvin would answer politely, but Lemell was snarky and didn't care if my itty-bitty feelings were hurt. She seemed strong enough to handle every aspect of life, but the subject of Jacquelyn Studevent rubbed her in a way I found puzzling. I noticed that Momma always lit a cigarette whenever the subject of my mother came up and she often went on a rant.

"Calvin, don't talk to me about that drug-addicted White woman who abandoned her own child. And by the way, why is she even using the last name Studevent? Did that crazy nigga' Raymond secretly marry her? He is already married. That nephew is crazy, but he ain't stupid. He brought himself right back to this side of town and married a Black woman. He realized that Black women ain't half bad, after all. That White woman wants to be a nigga so bad she is sleeping with our men, having Black babies. Yeah, you, Raymond Jr., you a nigga, too, just like your sorry daddy! Blue eyes and all, just read your birth certificate! That floozy even named her other child after a Black school. Howard. Boy, your daddy ain't give you nothing but his name and she wants that, too!"

One night, after I got off the phone with my mother, I sensed Lemell's irritation. I reassured her that I loved her and Calvin and had no desire to go back with my mother.

How could a six or seven-year-old child be so sensitive to another person's feelings? I had been hurt and disappointed a great deal, so I cherished any relationship and cared deeply for anyone who showed me any measure of love and decency. When a person has been through what I'd experienced, you know what hurt looks like and you can sense it because you are always on the lookout and honestly expecting it.

That evening, after a quiet dinner, my sisters and I washed the dishes and headed off to bed. I walked into Momma's room, where she was rolling her hair. Calvin appeared to be asleep. I kneeled down and began to say my prayers. Toward the end, I uttered a cluster of words that by Momma's reaction you would have thought I was praying to Satan the Devil.

"And God, can you please help my real mother get better from being sick. She is a good person but she has some problems. Can you please help her? And…"

At this point, Momma interrupted me so I tried to wrap things up quickly. "Amen!" I said. "Amen and goodnight!"

Then Momma unloaded on me.

"Boy, as long as you are breathing in this house, eating my food, sleeping under my roof, kneeling down on my floor, wearing pajamas that I bought and praying to my God, don't you ever mention that so-called mother of yours in this house. Oh, I am sorry, your 'real' mother!"

Calvin woke up, jumped out of bed, picked me up, and while he held me he insisted that I not shed a tear.

"Remember big man, Studevent men don't cry."

He calmly turned to Momma.

"Lemell, what is your problem?"

In a home of Black folks, when one is addressed by their full name, it usually means they have made a big mistake or committed a grave sin. That was probably the first and only time I recall Calvin addressing her as Lemell and not Baby.

"Why are you taking your anger toward the folks in Mississippi and his mother out on this boy? This is a God-fearing church going home and love is always in order. How do explain praying to God to forgive people for sins and he sees you hating on folks because they mistreated you as a child? That boy didn't choose to come into this world, and he didn't choose to be born into that ghetto. Now if you ask me, you need to drop to your knees and ask God to forgive you for unloading on this child like that. And you are not above apologizing to him yourself. You think he wants to worship the same God that we do if we ain't no different than them folks on the other side of the bridge?"

Like I said, Calvin was my hero. He did not micro-manage the house. He set a tone of love, respect, fun and laughter. Anything that threatened those things he dealt with firmly and immediately, even if that included his beloved wife, Lemell.

Story #3—Greaster Sunday, The Church Choir, and Raymond Sr.

As soon as she is fully awake, I am dying to tell Momma the story about an Easter Sunday that became one of the most incredible days of my life. Up until then, Calvin bailed me out on many occasions by playing the "boys will be boys" card. Lemell would respond with "Black mommas will be Black mommas" because she had decided that the honeymoon was over for this "rambunctious lil' blue-eyed devil." Once she discovered that I held my head over the stove to pretend to have a fever in order to miss church, even Calvin, who found it rather funny, couldn't save me from going to church. Momma hatched a new plan to help me expend my seemingly endless energy in a way that suited her.

She learned about an audition for the junior church choir to be held on Easter Sunday and arranged for me to sing in front of everyone with the incredible senior choir. She knew the choir director liked to see which kids could sing in front of people without getting nervous. What better way to find out who was not afraid of the big moment than to have a young one sing in front of an entire congregation of more than five hundred Black folks on Easter Sunday.

Unbeknownst to me, Baptist churches like to show off their choirs to pastors from other churches, especially ones from other cities, so having a seven-year-old lil' white Negro boy step up to the microphone could either go well or embarrass the reverend. Momma was more concerned about the Studevent name being tainted but she'd heard me sing around the house and thought I had potential. Much to my chagrin, she retracted that statement years later and told me that I couldn't sing a lick, but she needed something to calm my hyper self down.

To avoid any potential embarrassment, Momma got someone to help me. Calvin came home one day and introduced me to a woman he called Aunt Connie. That's when I learned how Black people refer to some as "aunt" or "uncle" when they don't want children to know the truth behind family secrets or when something is too complicated to understand.

I hadn't seen Aunt Connie before, but I wasn't about to forget her anytime soon. She was a beautiful mocha brown woman with a gorgeous complexion, the first woman I had ever seen with sparkling, smiling eyes. She also had a warm, motherly tenderness about her that left an indelible impression upon me. Her voice was raspy and sounded strained from so much singing, but once she opened her mouth, it was clear that her voice was still incredible.

Her real name was Connie Christmas. In 1962, at the age of sixteen, she made a name for herself with a trio of classic hits, such as "What a Night," "Big Chief," and "Tell It Like It Is." You can check her out on YouTube, Connie Christmas, to get an idea.

The plot thickened when I learned how "Aunt Connie" was related. Whenever she came over, she brought a darling, shy cute little girl, named Yolanda. After a few weeks, several people commented that she had a striking resemblance to me, that both of us have that Studevent gap in our teeth. As it turned out, Yolanda is my biological father's daughter and Connie Christmas was her mother.

I loved when Aunt Connie referred to me as Baby and Sugar and I knew I would be ready come Easter. I was too young to realize the magnitude of what was about to take place, but she made me feel as though I was ready to blow the doors off that church.

"Listen, Baby, when the choir director calls your name, walk slowly and say a quick prayer to the Lord. You ask the man upstairs, 'Lord, I know this is your house and you own it, but for the next three minutes can I have permission to own the mic?' The Lord will no doubt answer you, and Sugar, with the Lord blowing air in your lil' lungs, you ain't got nothin' to worry about. And then you know what I want your little seven-year-old lungs to do for Aunt Connie? I want you to close those big, beautiful blue eyes and give them Black folks an Easter Sunday they won't ever forget. Let them uppity Negroes have it."

Because I had been through so many traumatic events, I had no reason to be nervous. Aunt Connie had no idea how much it meant to me that she didn't resent my devilish blue eyes. That woman made me believe I could sing, but before I had a chance to utter a single note, Momma nearly killed me for a terrible mishap that lived in infamy in the Studevent family.

The big day finally arrived, and Calvin and Lemell had one of their few disagreements that morning over what gospel singer we should listen to: Mahalia Jackson or Marian Anderson. Mahalia was the queen of gospel at the time, although Aretha Franklin lovers might argue. Many historians would argue that Mahalia helped open the door for folks like Aretha. Either way, Calvin wanted to listen to Marian Anderson, while the girls preferred Mahalia Jackson.

Calvin was proud of any accomplishment colored folks had made and reminded us that when he was a twelve-year-old boy growing up in Washington, DC, an important event in the history of Black people had taken place. In early 1939, Marian Anderson, an incredible opera singer, was denied the right to sing at Constitution Hall. President Roosevelt and his wife Eleanor insisted that Marian be allowed to sing on Easter Sunday. So, on April 9, 1939, Marian Anderson sang in front of 75,000 people on the steps of the Lincoln Memorial. Millions around America tuned in to listen to her light up the sky with her incredible voice.

Calvin recalled going down to the mall to hear her sing.

"I could hear her blowing from four blocks away. Looking back, I hate the hypocrisy because she opened up singing *America*, the same place that wouldn't allow a Black woman to sing. So guys, Marian Anderson will always have a place in my heart on Easter Sunday."

How could Lemell, a Southern Black woman, argue with his reasoning? However, when we came home from church, it was Mahalia's voice that came through the static filled speakers. Had they asked me, Aunt Connie Christmas would have gotten my vote.

The house was immaculate because we were hosting the reverend and the guest pastor and his entourage from Chicago later that evening. We had spent the day before scrubbing the house top to bottom. I helped Calvin wax the car, and even though we walked to church, the sparkling gold Cadillac Coupe De Ville had to be spotless so folks could marvel at it, sitting there in the driveway like it was on display in a museum.

Everyone was excited because Momma was cooking her legendary fried chicken. For Black folks to prefer eating a fried chicken dinner on Easter instead of traditional turkey and ham says it all about her cooking.

Unbeknownst to this little white Negro, chicken grease was Momma's secret ingredient for chicken and her scrumptious gravy. We lived next door to the church, so we walked platters full of chicken and bowls of gravy over to the dining hall. What I didn't know back in those days was that Black folks kept three types of grease on the stove: bacon grease, fish grease, and chicken grease, plus a can of Crisco. Grease cans are a staple in any Southern Black woman's kitchen and Momma didn't mind crediting the segregated South with teaching her that.

We were dressed a touch sharper than usual that morning. Momma was dressed to kill, with white gloves up to her elbows and a white hat to match. After we took one last look in the mirror, the Studevent clan gathered at the door. This was probably the first moment when I felt I must be Black. Cadillacs. Chocolate City. Fried chicken. Collard greens. Sweet potato pies. Dressed to impress. Singing in a Baptist church choir. Now I knew I was Black for sure. That was also the day I started walking with a stroll.

Calvin and I were standing in the yard, marveling at the shine on the "'Lac," as Calvin called it.

"Cookie, Mell, come on Baby, let's go."

"I can't find my grease!"

Calvin was bewildered because Momma, Linda, and Cookie had already greased their scalps the night before with what was known as Blue Magic hair grease.

"Did any of you move the three cans of grease that were on top of the stove?"

Realizing what cans Momma was referring to, I was tempted to lie. However, with all the talk during the week about how Jesus died for our sins so we can be forgiven, I thought I had better speak up. When Momma looked at me, her motherly instincts kicked in. In an Alfred Hitchcock type tone, she gazed up at the sky, as if to ask the Lord to keep her calm.

"Raymond Lorenzo Studevent, Jr., look at me."

In my enthusiasm to clean the house, I had inadvertently thrown out Lemell's grease cans. Cookie had set them by the trash can while she scrubbed the stove top. I thought they were trash so I threw them out with the car cleaning materials, which meant they couldn't be salvaged.

"Did you throw away the three cans that were on top of the stove?"

My eyes filled with tears and I tried to put on the saddest face I could. I also attempted to use my scratchy throat from all the singing rehearsals, complete with a fake cough, hoping to appeal to any ounce of sympathy she might have.

"Yes, Ma'am," I whispered.

My ploy didn't work, and Momma went ballistic. Just as she asked what I did with the bacon grease, we heard Cookie yelling from inside the house.

"Momma, why is the kitchen sink clogged up?"

When I told Momma that I had poured the bacon grease down the kitchen sink, I thought she would have a heart attack. Needless to say, the sink got clogged. If Jesus died for our sins, I suppose Momma felt as though I had used up my allotment of forgiveness and deserved to die.

"Lord Jesus, I know it's your death, but I am about to kill this little blue-eyed rascal and send him home to you!"

That Easter came to be known as "Greaster Sunday!"

Thank God it happened on a day when Momma felt the spirit of God in her soul; otherwise we would have been attending church for my funeral. Fortunately, the only woman that Momma trusted with chicken grease was Connie, the one true queen of fried chicken. She brought her chicken grease over, and later that evening, the folks from Chicago were ready to lick their plates. If she wasn't already by then, Aunt Connie became my first childhood crush for sure when she rescued me from the grease.

With that resolved, it was time to get to The Upper Room Baptist Church and enjoy the spectacle and the festivities, with none bigger than my upcoming turn at the microphone.

Easter Sunday was a time to dress to impress. I knew Easter had something to do with the death and resurrection of Jesus, but it seemed to be more of a fashion show than anything else. The only thing dying I could see was a bunch of Black women dying to get out of those heels that were killing their feet. When I looked under the seats, all the folks had their shoes off. But up top, it was like a convention of proud peacock and I couldn't even see the pulpit through all the large, bright colored hats.

Older women put the younger ones to shame when it came time to pull it together for the good Lord. They wore suits in every color of the rainbow: pink, purple, gold, lime green, and orange. The showstopper? One woman with the courage to wear a white-on-white ensemble.

Just like an iceberg, there was more under the surface. Women wore undergarments to hold stuff in place. Girdles, corsets, slips, brassieres, and body liners kept everything tight, especially when the swaying began. Even though we were filled with the unbridled joy of the resurrection, with Jesus rising from the grave and granting us all eternal life, it was an unwritten rule that you did not hug a woman on Easter Sunday. Otherwise, you might disrupt her perfectly strategized arrangement.

Not to be outdone, the men brought out all their best accessories—tie clips, cuff links, collar bars, and tie pins engraved with their initials. You could be certain that the tie was not going to budge even a millimeter with all those things holding it in place. Whether or not to wear a hat was not even a question. The issue was how to tilt the brim just right as to be slightly cool, but not mimic a street hustler and offend the Lord in his house of worship. Of course, if you weren't sure about the angle, there would be an older Black woman available to straighten you up. For me, Easter meant I always got a new suit with a tie and hankie to match.

The biggest celebrity in nearly every Black neighborhood was the reverend, with his ability to motivate people to do right in the eyes of God. Of course, those same people needed to allow the Holy Ghost to compel them to reach inside their purses and wallets to not only keep the doors of the church open, but to pay for the reverend to keep a brand spanking new Cadillac in the parking lot. On Easter Sunday, everybody gave just a little bit more because they wanted the Lord to know they appreciated the sacrifice made for their sins to be forgiven.

The second most popular person in these neighborhoods was the lead singer in the Baptist church choir. Many great artists began their career singing in their local church choir, like Marvin Gaye (DC Native), Aretha (Refa) Franklin, Diana Ross, and Whitney Houston.

Calvin was a Deacon, so he took a position near the door, assisting older folks to their seats. I was beginning to get nervous about my solo. When I went to the restroom, I heard a friend's father tell his son, "Don't let that White boy out blow you."

"White boy?" my friend said. "Daddy, his name is Raymond."

Connie had overheard visitors in the restroom instructing their daughters that, "No matter what, y'all can't allow that curly head White boy win."

I was so disappointed that even as a child in the church, I was not exempt from the disdain some Black folks had for White people. My nerves calmed down once I caught sight of Aunt Connie. Momma took her seat in the choir section. Calvin walked me to my seat and resumed his post. To my surprise, Aunt Connie came up and handed me a throat lozenge.

"Sugar, keep this in the back of your mouth, but no matter what, don't swallow it. Baby, no matter what happens, I am proud of you. Now you know what to do."

I shoved that lozenge in my mouth.

"Sugar, I know, let 'em have it."

She smiled.

"Boy, did you call me Sugar?"

"I'm so sorry, Ma'am. I meant to call you by your full name, 'Brown Sugar.'"

She gave me a hug and we laughed.

Momma began swaying back and forth as the choir warmed up. They wanted the visitors to take word back to Chicago that them folks down in Chocolate City can "sang."

I was so nervous, everything seemed magnified. The church gave warm welcoming applause to the invited reverend from Chicago. I stood up, afraid to look at Momma because of the grease incident. To make things worse, I had accidentally swallowed my lozenge and was trying to punch my chest to get it to move down my throat.

After the first sermon, they called the first couple kids to audition. They were pretty good, and I looked at Aunt Connie for reassurance. Momma always looked up at the sky when she sang, almost as if she wanted to make sure the Lord heard her in heaven. I couldn't take my eyes off the microphone. I could hear Connie's words loud and clear, "Own the mic."

Then the moment of truth arrived. As the organ quieted, and the choir began a soft hum, the reverend yelled, "Raymond, come up and testify to the congregation how you feel and more importantly, tell the Lord how blessed you feel!"

I cleared my throat, whispered a quick prayer and followed Connie's directions not to sing the words right away but to first show my range with an old trick she taught me to kill the nerves and give the impression I was a "real" singer. She knew that I knew the vowels of the alphabet, A, E, I, O and U. She had me falsetto harmonize those and when I got to the letter U, I would sing it as the word, "You," in reference to the Lord.

It started well, with a few folks shouting the usual Baptist Church chants, such as, "Go on boy," and "Sing the song!"

The day had started out awful, and just when I thought it could not get any worse, it did. To my surprise, my biological father and Connie's estranged husband showed up in the middle of my solo. The sight of him totally threw my concentration. My voice cracked and I stormed out from behind the pulpit, catching him halfway down the aisle. His breath smelled like a distillery and he was slurring his words, obviously drunk. Calvin stepped to him and asked him to leave. He had never cared anything about my well-being and that day was no different. He was not there to support me or to hear me sing. He was following Connie.

"You thought you could hide from me?" he yelled. "You trying to keep my daughter from me! Look, you so-called church people, two of my kids are in here and nobody wants me to see them. I'm their daddy!"

Calvin removed his blazer and signaled to the other deacons that things were about to escalate.

Raymond told the reverend off as well.

"You don't do anything but rip these people off, Mr. Reverend. Look! This little White boy, that's my kid. Y'all uppity Negroes trying to take him away from me."

He looked at me and took out his driver's license.

"Look boy, that's your name right here, Raymond Studevent. I gave you my name."

By this time, Momma had walked down from the choir.

"Negro, you gave him your name, but that's all you gave him."

Raymond laughed and looked at Calvin

"Where you find this country Mississippi nigga at?"

Calvin wrapped his arms around his brother, picked him up and walked him out the front door of the church. The choir director tried to be helpful and get things back on track by rushing me back to the pulpit. In my misdirected anger, I let him have a piece of my mind.

"Is that what this church thing is all about? Black people singing all these songs about love? The moment somebody looks a little different, you treat them like an outsider. I ain't no fool. I know that they are really singing Negro spiritual songs that came mostly from slaves. I'm young, but I read about twenty-five books a month. You folks ain't no better than them White people. Look up there, isn't that something? A picture of a White Jesus. Make up your minds, Black folks. You want a solo? Well, here's a little something to chew on!"

The other trick I learned from Connie about singing in the choir was that the uglier the face you made while singing, the easier it was to give the impression that you were filled with the Holy Ghost. With that in mind, I twisted my face as if I had taken a bite into the sour skin of a lemon. I started to sing the Negro national anthem, "Lift Every Voice and Sing." I sang like an angel and blew everyone's mind.

The director said that it wasn't a church song.

"That's because you people ain't acting like church folks," I said.

Later that day, back home enjoying Momma's legendary fried chicken, the reverend offered me the choir position. I told Momma I didn't want to do it because I felt like the people in the church were Black racists, no different than White folks. She explained that many of the church members were from the South, just like her, and had grown up during difficult times in the days of segregation.

When Momma wakes up, I know she will certainly recall this story.

Story #4—Black Television Shows and Movies

Like a lot of folks back then, we only had one TV set, a small black-and-white model. Considering how nice the house was decorated and how classy the cars were, I was surprised at this setup. Calvin didn't think we should spend a lot of time sitting in front of a box. He felt it was a colossal waste when there were so many other, more important things to do.

We watched *Soul Train* every Saturday morning. One day, the entire family started yelling, "Refa, look at that Refa!" I was aware that the word "reefer" was a synonym for marijuana. I also knew that Calvin and Momma hated drugs. I found out quick that it wasn't reefer madness. Everyone was mesmerized by Refa, as in Aretha Franklin, the Queen of Soul, who had a guest appearance on the show.

Was I hearing things? In the world known as Ebonics, the letters "th" are sometimes pronounced like an "f," so "Aretha" was pronounced "Arefa." Saturday morning television was my introduction into the world of Black slang. I was learning to read and this grammatical "rule" seemed reasonable since "ph" is pronounced like "f." Besides, Calvin, Momma, and Linda all worked in the library system so why would I ever question them regarding the English language?

As I began to settle in and get more comfortable, I started to needle Cookie because I thought she was prejudiced against White people, and therefore me. I would intentionally say that I thought Marcia from *The Brady Bunch* was much prettier than Thelma from *Good Times*. It didn't take long for her to unleash a fury of Black pride.

"In *this* house, we only got one television, and we only watch Black shows, like *Good Times, The Jeffersons, Sanford and Son, Soul Train,* not corny White folks' shows, like *American Bandstand.* Maybe

Welcome Back Kotter because they got a brother on there and that Vinnie Barbarino White boy is kinda cute."

One night, Cookie said, "Momma, come watch *King Kong* with us."

Momma stopped dead in her tracks.

"Child please. That's the most racist movie I've ever seen. Some big black ape going crazy over some blue-eyed, blonde heifer. All them jungle niggers jumping around, worshipping her like she some Greek goddess. Where do you think the terms 'jungle fever' and 'going ape' come from?"

"Momma, the television is black-and-white so how do you know she has blue eyes?"

She looked at me and walked away. I began to irritate Momma when I reminded her that we had recently watched *Planet of the Apes* and a White man had kissed a female ape.

"Momma, what's wrong with a Black ape falling in love with a White woman and a White man falling in love with a Black ape?"

Life always seemed to revolve around the issue of race. It was exhausting. It seemed as though every time I stepped out the door a potential confrontation was awaiting. Maybe I blew these thoughts way out of proportion, but not a day went by that I didn't feel like an "undercover brother," and the issue of race never left me.

Story #5—Momma's Thoughts on Racism

Some of life's most precious moments occur when an unexpected gift is given at a most unexpected time. I received such a gift during one of the worst blizzards to ever hit our area, when I was the only one left living with Momma in her house. We were stranded for several days so we binge watched movies, like *The Color Purple*, *Mississippi*

Burning, and *A Time to Kill.* If we hadn't gotten burned out, we would have watched the epic saga *Roots,* yet again.

Momma actually lived those stories and had a front row seat for much of the madness. She knew that Claudette Colvin was actually the original Rosa Parks. A few months before the infamous bus episode, the courageous and headstrong fifteen-year-old Claudette was arrested in Montgomery, Alabama, for refusing to give up her seat to a White woman. Although Momma had already left Mississippi, she said the reason everyone kept silent down South about Claudette was because she was pregnant. Face it, a fifteen-year-old pregnant Black girl wasn't exactly a shining example for Black folks. If advertised, it would only feed into the stereotype that Black folks were lazy, oversexed and undisciplined. Claudette was also dark-skinned. According to Momma, the reason Rosa Parks got more attention was because she was light-skinned and didn't have nappy hair.

Momma also said that during the Civil Rights movement many Black folks decided to use the light-skinned Thurgood Marshall, Cab Calloway, Lena Horne, Joe Louis complexion effect to try to improve their lot in life. All of them were supposedly able to make headway in the struggle for racial equality solely because they were light-skinned and considered less threatening to the White establishment. She explained that soon after, the Black Panthers and Malcolm X had other ideas about how Black folks needed to take what they wanted "by any means necessary." Her reminders of what it was like for her and others during the segregated South always made me quite sad.

For the duration of the storm, our favorite time of day became four o'clock in the afternoon when *The Oprah Winfrey Show* aired. Momma got me hooked on it, just like her. She used to joke that Black folks are always late so Oprah had to air her show in the afternoon.

"White people like *Good Morning America* because they get up early. They can't have a show called *Good Morning Black People*. They need to have a show called *Good Afternoon Black Folks*. Of course it wouldn't start until after lunch because we ain't getting up to watch no talk show with them interviewing a bunch of rich celebrities making us feel poor."

Let the record show that Black folks coined the phrase "ish" to establish a sense of time. Seven-ish means just before eight o'clock. Even the television show *black-ish* means it might start late.

"Ain't no Black woman getting up at three o'clock in the morning to do a 6:00 AM show!" Momma said. "We gotta do our hair, shoot, ain't no way! Oprah could do it back when she had her Afro and she didn't have to do her hair. Boy, that Oprah is smart. She straightened her hair out and then she got that television show. That Afro scared White people when she was in Baltimore because I used to see her doing local reports from the ghetto. White folks ain't sending none of their people into an all-Black neighborhood. 'Send the Black woman with the Afro because they will talk to her instead of beating her up.' She straightened them naps out and them TV folks were like Bob Barker on the *Price is Right*, 'Come on Down!' "

One thing I learned from Momma was that conversation about hair with a Black woman can go really bad, really fast. That conversation led to a lesson on my own hair. She always told me to lose the curls and straighten my hair so I could look as White as possible. This was confusing for me as a youngster because she always reminded me that I was Black, but when it came time to make it in this world it was best to sometimes play the White card. Her feelings about me doing that often depended on her mood.

Years later, I recall Momma being concerned that Obama might embarrass Black folks by being late for his inauguration.

"Shoot, Michelle ain't gonna let Barrack be late. She's gonna wake him up early that morning and say, 'Look, Mr. Newly-Elected President, I helped you get here so don't embarrass me. There's a lot of excited Black folks coming out in that cold weather to celebrate. Some took off work, some will get fired, and some will ask you for a job if they get close enough.'"

Momma was so proud about Barack being married to a Black woman. She said that he wouldn't have become president without a strong Black woman at his side, lifting him up in a way a White woman could not. She respected many White women, and *The Golden Girls* was one of her favorite shows. For a long time, she thought Estelle Getty was the White version of Aunt Esther from *Sanford and Son*. As she got older, her stance became more pro-Black than anti-White.

Momma admired strong women of all races, though, especially the classy ones. She had the utmost respect for Jackie O. She was a huge fan of the fashion designer Chanel because of her name. Even though she could never afford to buy any Chanel pieces, Momma loved the name Coco. In her mind, she thought Chanel had to be a Black woman because with a name like Coco, what else could she be?

There was even a time that Momma thought Mother Nature was Black. We used to joke that when she was tired of going to work, Mother Nature would help out Black folks by creating a snowstorm so they could stay home and relax for a couple days. I asked her if Father Time was a White man because he was responsible for so much death.

"No. Eve ate that apple and that's why we dying at eighty-years old. I'm sure Eve was a White woman because if a Black woman heard a snake talking, she'd run so fast the apple would have turned into apple sauce by the time she stopped!"

Momma's opinion of Black men was a little different. One day, she told me a story about Sidney Poitier and Harry Belafonte.

"It was 1959. I was in my twenties, working in the library. The latest edition of *Ebony* magazine hit the shelves and Sidney Poitier was on the cover with his beautiful Black wife, Juanita. The caption read: *First Negro Movie Star*. Boy, were we proud! Whoa! Sidney was dark chocolate fine!"

Then her tone abruptly changed.

"But just like old calypso Harry, they both couldn't wait to dump their Black wives and marry a White woman. The part that makes me sad is that the Black wife supports her husband through his lean, tough years. She gives him a few children while he provides a nice celebrity lifestyle. But once the kids become self-sufficient, these Black husbands want to move on. The Black wife never gets to enjoy the marriage because she sacrificed the early years supporting her husband and raising their kids, often putting her dreams or aspirations on hold. When they are divorced, she gets alimony but by then she's in her forties and has to look for a career. The man she helped to mature dumps her and a White woman benefits from all her hard work. That's why you never see any of these brothers sitting together at awards ceremonies. Deep down inside, they are ashamed of each other."

She dug in further on Harry Belafonte.

"I remember seeing him on these magazine covers, once in Africa holding a baby acting as though he was still in the fight for us. He fought for civil rights, but you never saw him out there with his wife, and all Black women knew why. You never saw those Black men on the cover of magazines with their White wives. Everybody always telling them they look so lean and trim. That's because they hungry, sitting there dying for some collared-greens, ham hocks and neck bones. Done moved to Hollywood, starved for some soul food. Out there eating tofu, soy, gluten-free whatever. Negro please. Child, you would never see real brothers like Muhammad Ali, Marvin Gaye, or Smokey Robinson do something like that."

Even though Momma laughed sometimes, I knew she felt bad for the women who worked hard to support those men.

"Yeah they realized Black women ain't taking none of that celebrity nonsense. Quincy Jones did the same thing. O. J. went from running through airports for Hertz to running away from his first wife only to start dating a seventeen-year-old White girl."

During the trial she gave me a history lesson on O. J.

"I remember it like yesterday. It was the November 1976 issue of *Ebony* magazine. O. J. was on the cover with his beautiful wife, Marguerite, and their two kids. The next year, he left his family for a White teenage waitress who had just graduated high school. The girl was too young to even bring him a drink. Marguerite stuck by O. J. in college, gave him two kids, and as soon as he got some money, he left her to raise them young beauties by herself. Well, he sure found out now that being with a White woman don't make you White."

In a matter of seconds, Momma came up with another one of her classic lines.

"Yeah, he played running back alright. But now he's running back to us Black folks. Next, he will come into the courtroom barefoot, wearing an African dashiki and a bone through his nose."

She was on a roll.

"You ain't never heard of no rich Black woman dating a teenage waiter right out of high school. Black women marry rich White men, like them sisters who married George Lucas and Robert De

Niro. Diana Ross and Tina Turner did it the best way. They went to Europe and got a rich White man from the old country. They did it Jackie O style. Their White husbands get described with words Black folks can't even relate to, like tycoon, magnate, mogul. Sure beats O. J.'s waitress!"

Despite the issue of race being the most polarizing issue in America, Momma didn't only lambast iconic brothers from days gone by. Current brothers of today weren't exempt from her wrath, in particular Tiger Woods.

"Wow, that boy didn't even give a Black woman a chance. At least O. J. and the other brothers married a sister first. True, O. J. married a waitress, but this fool Tiger done married a babysitter."

"Momma, she was a nanny."

"Psst, Negro please, a nanny ain't nothin' but White folks fancy word for babysitter. Tiger got millions, went to Stanford and the best he can do is a diaper changer! These Black men will do anything for a White woman. For their wedding vows, Tiger says, 'When I saw you change that diaper and mix that milk formula, I knew you were the one.' Then stupid O. J. 'My dear, when you poured the white cream in my black coffee I knew it was a sign that we should be together.'"

I was laughing so hard I just egged her on.

"Momma, Tiger says he ain't Black."

By then, she was in silly Black woman mode.

"Yeah nigga talkin' about he being Caberasian or Cameroonian or some ol' crazy name. He a nigga just like us."

Wanting to hear more, I kept stirring the pot.

"He said he really don't know what he is."

"Oh, I can help Tiger find out who he is. They got a special program down South to help lost, mixed up, half-breed Negroes find themselves. All Mr. Tiger gotta do is drive that White girl through Mississippi. Them hillybilly policemen down there will be more than happy to help Mr. Woods find out what he is. If he thinks that golf club the White girl put on him was somethin' just wait til' he ride through 'Crackerville,' Mississippi. They'll turn him into 'Kitten' Woods."

We were both dying from laughter.

"'I'm Tiger sir.' 'You who boy? Tiger? Listen Tyrone, down here I'm the Lion King, nigger. Now you look like a New Orleans Creole boy or what yo' folks call 'passin.' That's your new name boy, 'Passin', as in passin' through Mississippi. Keep it movin' now 'cause New Orleans is straight west, Tyrone.'"

Momma's sweet revenge came on Friday nights when she snuck in a peek at her secret White man crush. I teased her because she loved to watch *Magnum, P.I.* with Tom Selleck and Burt Reynolds in *Cannonball Run*. She even said that Loni Anderson, Burt's wife, was one lucky woman. But after watching *Butch Cassidy and the Sundance Kid*, her main White man crush became clear. When I told her that all the ladies loved Robert Redford, she leaned back in her chair and gave me that look.

"I don't care about no Robert Redford. You'd better believe if that Butch fellow Paul Newman came knocking at my door, I might have to sell myself out. Boy, that is one good looking White man. He even had a Black man's name, Butch. Raymond, don't tell anybody you heard me say that about that fine White man."

"Well, too bad Paul Newman has those devilish blue eyes."

"No he doesn't, his eyes are brown."

I couldn't prove my point without a color television, so I used the opportunity to push for a new set so we could settle the issue.

After joking about having no more white food in the house, she snuck in some Paul Newman salad dressing one time. She respected Denzel Washington and Paul Newman because they stuck with the woman who helped them achieve their dreams. They hadn't made it in Hollywood and started chasing every woman in sight.

I often used the Paul Newman salad dressing and other racially friendly episodes as an excuse to stir the pot regarding me marrying a White woman.

"Momma, since Paul Newman seems to have the green light in this house, it would appear that you are softening your feelings toward White people. Does that mean that me being half-White affords me the liberty to marry a White woman, if I kind of accidentally find one and I just trip and fall in love?"

"Boy you need to go to Sudan, Uganda or somewhere in the Blackest jungle in Africa. Tell them right before you enter that you are the new Tarzan and you want the Blackest woman you can find. We simply can't afford any more of these genetic mishaps giving us white Negroes like you. It takes too much work to stand here and call you a Negro while you stare back at me with those devilish blue eyes and straight hair. Now, take a flight to Africa and make this thing right by bringing home a sister from the Motherland. She needs to be so Black that when you bring her into my house, she sets off my smoke alarm. So Black that she pees coffee! None of this Camille Cosby, Debbie Allen, Lena Horne, or Jasmine Guy nonsense. Bring home Kizzy from *Roots*, Harriet Tubman or somebody like that! Spooky Juice African funky Original Nappy Black Negroid!"

All joking aside, Momma expressed her feelings about the importance of Black fathers and positive role models in the success of Black children. She pointed out the success of modern-day athletes, such as Michael Jordan, Tiger, and the Williams sisters. They are arguably the greatest to ever play their sports and the one common denominator is that they had a strong father.

Momma also never trusted men in positions that gave them access to children. She felt teachers, Boy Scout leaders, priests and coaches should be watched carefully. She suspected many of them of being pedophiles and sadly she was right too many times.

Her pro-Black opinions were made evident one time when I was young and she walked in the house while I was watching a famous Black boxer out of Cuba, named Teófilo Stevenson. He had won three Olympic gold medals and had a striking resemblance to Muhammad Ali.

"Go ahead Ali, knock that boy out!"

I told her that he was a Cuban who didn't even speak English. I suggested she should root for the American boxer and she went international on me.

"He's Black and the other man is White, so I root for the brother. The only difference between him and Ali is that his slave ship went south, and Ali's went north."

I explained to her that Stevenson could not turn pro because Cuban President Fidel Castro would not allow athletes to do that.

"Cuba ain't no different than America. White man holding a good-looking Black boxer down. They ruined Ali's career and that Cuban brother got the same treatment. Like I said, knock him out!"

For some reason, *Star Wars* always conjured up excitement in Momma. Nothing was funnier than her comparison between my life and that of Luke Skywalker. Of course, the laughs centered around my racial makeup.

"That's why Luke Skywalker had a Black father. It's like Dark Vader is your Black father and you're the White Luke Skywalker."

When I corrected her and explained that his name was "Darth" and not "Dark," she defended her words.

"Well, in my book he's 'Dark' because he acts just like your dark daddy. He wasn't in his son's life for years and then he got the nerve to show up talking foolish. 'Luke, I'm yo' daddy.' Psst! Nigga please!"

I cracked up.

"My daddy? Fool, I ain't seen you in light years and you come around here talking about you being my daddy."

Momma drove it home.

"Even in Hollywood, they got the Black man in outer space being a deadbeat dad."

"Maybe we need to ask NASA if they can put me on the next shuttle rocket so I can go find my daddy."

5

"Boy, when are you going to get it through your thick White skull that I ain't your momma?"

After perusing through my memory for nearly an hour, I felt prepared to shower Momma with some of the most memorable moments in our lives. As soon as she woke up, I was absolutely sure that after telling her the "Greaster Sunday" story and the others, she would remember that I was her adopted son and we could finally be done with this nonsense. Not only did I not get to share the stories with her; she made it clear that she was ready for me to leave.

"You still here, White man?"

"Yeah, I was hoping to spend this Saturday evening sharing some more stories with you."

"Saturday, I thought it was February. I have to get ready for church. Well, listen, I hate to be rude, White man, but I've got to get my clothes ready for church. The van picks me up at seven o'clock sharp, and I can't be late. They got church service at this place, but they ain't got no choir, and I love to sing my praises to the Lord. Hallelujah!"

I couldn't say a word.

"I have no idea why I'm telling you about Black folks' church, because I'm sure you don't know a thing about the Lord and his relationship with Black folks. See, the man upstairs loves to hear us Negroes sing. That's why he gave us a choir. On your side of town, you got the Glee Club. Oh, no, you call it the 'chorus.' The one that kills me is when White folks try to get away with calling it an 'ensemble.' Listen to me; I'm just talking and talking. You're starting to be a bad influence on me. You got me babbling foolishness, just like White folks do. Well, don't stand there looking like a fool. Help me up so I can get to the closet."

I figured I might as well capitalize on her spiritual high to get her to remember our days together in the church, hoping she'd remember her son.

"White boy, what you know about the church?"

She dared me to sing a song from my days of attending. It had been a while, but I began belting out the words to "Go Tell It on the Mountain" until Momma started laughing.

"You White folks crack me up! That ain't no church song. That's an old Negro spiritual, sonny boy. Try again."

I started singing "Amazing Grace."

"Make up your mind, boy. First you want to take me back to slavery, and now you ready to bury me. What's next? You going to put me to work by singing 'I've Been Working on the Railroad'?"

As I looked through the church hymnbook, which happened to be laying on her nightstand, I recalled a song she loved, "What a Friend

We Have in Jesus." It was her favorite because Aretha Franklin sang it on one of her gospel albums.

"Tell me I don't know that you used to love that song when we sang it in church choir back in the day," I said, before I began to sing the first solo I ever had in church.

Momma pulled out a bright, violet-colored suit with matching gloves and a hat. She showed me a pair of purple suede shoes that were the same exact color of her suit.

"You like these? They are a size too small, but they were the only shoes the Chinese man had in this color. Don't matter because nobody can see my feet while I'm singing in my choir robe. My corns and bunions going to swell, but it's nothing some Epson salt can't fix."

"That's a real pretty violet you got there."

It seemed as though every conversation with Momma, past and present, ended up being about race and color.

"You can't possibly be related to me, because Black folks don't ever say 'violet.' That's a White folks' word. White folks always gotta complicate things. Purple is purple and orange is orange, not mango, coral, and what's that other one? Oh, yeah, apricot. It's orange. White folks really kill me when referring to the color white, 'cause you guys think it's necessary to come up with all these fancy shades of white, like ivory, bone, cream, eggshell, and pearl. Then, when you guys are feeling really bougie, y'all say something is as 'white as snow.' Y'all even got a Disney movie named after that Snow White, who is supposedly as pure as the driven snow."

"Why does everything have to be about black and white with you?"

She was on a roll, though, and didn't hear my question. Clearly irritated, she smacked her gums and yelled loud enough for anyone to hear.

"You don't ever hear all them fancy shades for the color black though, do you?

"No, you don't, but I've actually heard of the color flat black."

"*Hmmm,* that's 'cause we flat broke. You know what we say to that? *Psst,* nigga, please!"

I jumped up because once again she had referred to me as Black.

"Don't get excited cause I called you a nigga. Boy, when are you going to get it through your thick White skull that I *ain't* your momma?"

I quickly changed the conversation and decided to drop a quote I used to hear Calvin say to her whenever she was dressed up nice for church.

"Mell, Mell, Mell, you looking swell. Hey good looking, what you got cooking?"

She didn't respond.

"Do you remember Greaster Sunday, the time I threw away your grease cans?"

She smirked.

"Boy, the first thing a Black child is taught is to never touch the grease on the stove. I am going to pray for you tomorrow and hopefully the Lord will forgive you because you were probably an abused child or something like that. You know that stuff crazy White folks do."

She stopped her rant for a moment to catch her breath.

"I used to cook on Easter Sunday, back in the day."

I got so excited that I removed my glasses. Momma closed her eyes.

"Oh my God. Oh my Lord and Savior Jesus Christ. I don't believe this. I don't believe this!"

With tears welling up, I stuttered the word "Momma" just like Whoopi Goldberg's long-lost children did in *The Color Purple*. My hope for a Hollywood ending were quickly squashed when Momma looked up at me.

"I don't believe this! I don't have any purple pantyhose to match! Listen, White man, Black folks done served your people for many years, so now it's your turn to do something for us. You take one of these Goosey's and go find me some matching purple pantyhose. Don't come back here trying to be cute with some weird violet shade. I can't have that old uppity Sister Jackson thinking she can outdress me, 'cause Sista' Momma is the queen bee up in my church! You want me to be your momma? You do that for me, and you can call me your momma, your grandmomma, or your godmomma for all I care. It's raining outside, so you be sure not to let a single drop of water touch my Goosey's."

"Don't you mean Gucci's?"

"White boy, you making fun of me? White folks buy Gucci's, and I buy Goosey's from the Chinese folks who got the good fake stuff."

Before I left, I couldn't resist joking with her and asked a question that would surely have gotten me slapped in my youth.

"Would it be okay for me to get fishnet pantyhose if they don't have the plain smooth kind?"

Contrary to popular belief, most Black women I know get really quiet before they unleash their verbal wrath. Momma whispered a quick prayer through tightly clenched teeth.

"Lord, give me strength not to catch a murder case in my later years because I want to die under your terms."

Then she turned to me.

"Now, boy, I don't know where you got your ideas about Black women. Maybe because of the way these young floozies with no daddy go around with their chest hangin' out and pants so tight they look like they painted them on. I'm a God-fearing woman and don't you ever let me hear you suggest that I would wear the devil's fishnet pantyhose."

As I headed down the hall, I heard the door creak open. Momma stuck her head out and reminded me to protect her fake Gucci shoes.

"I don't want a single drop on my shoes, you hear? I gotta look good for church."

"Yes, Ma'am, I'm your son. I remember how you used to dress for church."

Not one to give a White person the last word, she let me have it.

"Boy, you gonna burn in hell for lying so much!"

6

"Please help me with my memory because I am forgetting so many things. Amen."

My quest for purple pantyhose led me on a drive through the streets of my childhood. I saw many changes, but one thing that remained the same was that almost every person I saw had well-groomed hair. Folks in DC had an obsession with their hair that was almost an addiction.

Despite the fact that Momma was getting on my nerves, cruising through the rugged streets of my old stomping grounds, reflecting back now on the early days, put me in a great mood. Possibly because I had just spent the previous few hours recalling some memorable moments of my life and even though I was not able to share them with Momma, they warmed my heart, nonetheless. At a light on the corner of Minnesota Avenue and Benning Road, I laughed at how we used to throw snowballs at city buses on that corner. The drivers would throw up their hands, as if to say, "Come on boys, let me see what you got." No doubt his bus had already been bombarded by some mischievous lads along his route.

Minnesota Avenue was a trip down memory lane. I also recalled the Bookmobile truck stopped there. I was destined to read books forever. Books! Books! Books! Lemell worked at the local library; Linda worked part-time at the same library to help pay for college, and Calvin drove the city's "library on wheels." Reading was a family affair, all right.

During my outing to pick up some violet, purple or lavender stockings, I had an epiphany. Those years were the happiest time of my life. I finally felt loved and cared for by a family who loved me, and while Lemell was a tough cookie at times, I felt the love that all children yearn for, with one sister who was fun to play games with and another who always caught me cheating at Monopoly.

Linda was the epitome of respect and cool, as illustrated in her explanation of "Black Power." We were eating ice cream, so she used our snack as a visual aid.

"Look in this bowl and watch what happens when I stir the chocolate ice cream with the weak vanilla ice cream," she said. "Notice how the ice cream turns all chocolate after the chocolate dominates the vanilla. That's Black Power."

"Well, what happened to me?"

She laughed.

"Well, you just came out of the toaster too early."

"Shucks, as White as I am, I don't even think the toaster was plugged in!"

Anytime we stepped outside our home, we carried ourselves "cool." Whether it was spelled with a C or a K, if I wanted to fit in, I needed to learn what it meant to be *cool*. I had been called "White boy" enough times to suspect that I had better embrace whatever this cool thing implied as soon as possible. If I were to have any chance of surviving, let alone find happiness, I had better be twice as cool as any Black person strutting his cool self down the avenue.

I used to hear Black folks talk about having soul power. While I understood that it meant a unity among Black folks, I could not explain its significance.

Soon after I moved to Momma's house, phrases like "What's up, cool breeze?" seemed to have replaced expressions like, "What it is, soul brother?" While the N-word was still popular, most of the guys referred to one another as "cool breeze" while loitering on the corner, doing what was effectively known as "cooling out." It seemed like every conversation between folks from the age of five to thirty centered on the word cool.

There was no social media or hip-hop music back then, but the latest fashion, slang, colloquialisms, and dances all spread like wildfire. Dances had weird names, such as The Bump, The Funky Chicken, The Bus Stop, The Rock and The Robot. Even The Hustle was accepted in our neighborhood.

Being cool was defined by your walk, talk, clothes, car, and above all else, your hair.

Kool brand cigarettes were the brand of choice, and the most popular drink was Kool-Aid. Funny thing about Kool-Aid is, nobody seemed to know the flavors, just the colors. Red was the all-time favorite, followed by purple, which I do recall being grape flavored.

Having a cool nickname was of the utmost importance. To this day, I don't think I ever knew the real names of half the people I grew up with. Unlike White people, who usually had nicknames derived from the person's real name—like Bob for Robert, Dick for Richard, or Tom for Thomas—people in my neighborhood had nicknames like Meatloaf, D. D., Beefrye, Knuckles, Porkchop, Duck, Bird, PoPo,

Meaty, Bo, and my favorite, Junebug. These names sounded more like the menu at a buffet.

There were no set rules, but by the age of five or six, most kids had already been christened with a nickname. If your family didn't give you one, then the neighborhood guys took care of it, based on your appearance. If you were skinny, you might be called Bones or Slim. Overweight kids had names, such as Fats, Fatboy or Chubby. If you were really dark-skinned, you might be called Sambo, Ace (as in the ace of spades) or simply Black.

I already had the nickname Scoop, but because I was so White kids in the neighborhood wanted to call me Ghost, Casper, and Salt. None of them stuck, and I stayed Scoop, which evolved from Scoot because I used to scoot across the floor, but as I got older I became Scoop, as in a scoop of vanilla ice cream. Silly, but true.

Girls had nicknames derived from dessert type food: Candy, Pumpkin, Honey, Pudding, Cookie, and my personal favorite, Peaches. Some girls had a short version of their real name, like Renee would be called Nay Nay and Shanice would be called Nee Nee.

My skin color was common conversation and I tried to ignore it but Linda and Cookie made it crystal clear that if I was going to fit in, I had to embrace the same foods, television shows, and even board games as they did. I did, but I always felt like the odd man out. Washington was known as "Chocolate City"—the Blackest city in America at the time—and I had landed like a sugar cube in a box of Milk Duds.

Most people believe that the best way to get a Black person to fight is to make an insult about his or her mother or use the N-word. The truth is, if you truly want to irritate a Black person, especially of the female persuasion, simply make a disparaging remark about her hair. She will unleash all her fury on you.

If you thought cooking grease was important, it couldn't compare to the significance of hair grease. Coconut oil often did the trick during an emergency, but somebody had better not ever use the last of the Ultra Sheen or Blue Magic hair grease. Finishing the Kool-Aid, especially the red, was bad, but not like using up the last bit of hair grease.

Besides the style, folks were fixated on hair texture, with an ongoing argument about "good hair" versus "bad hair," which was synonymous with nappy hair. Some folks felt compelled to claim that they had Indian blood in their DNA as a way of distancing themself from what some perceived to be a "Godforsaken, nappy, kinky, Brillo pad" atop one's head. Every girl, starting in first grade, took the baby hair along the edges of her face, coated it with baby oil and pressed it down along the side of her face. Even if she had coarse hair, she pressed it down and claimed that a distant relative was part Cherokee.

There might have been Native American DNA in some of these kids, but they didn't have my problems. Momma didn't trust the neighborhood barber shop because none of the barbers had experience cutting straight hair. My Black Power sisters, who were more like Hair Power Rangers, took up the challenge to make me look more Black. They thought that if I had a cool crop, I would blend in easier.

One day, Linda and Cookie came up with what they thought was a great idea.

"Let's give him a Jew perm."

I had no idea what that meant, but I did know that the guy in the Bible named Jesus was a Jew, and the most revered person in my house, so I was all for Cookie and Linda making me look like *him*.

Unlike the miracles performed by Jesus, my hairstyling session was a disaster. Momma almost fainted when she saw my crazy new do. The timing was bad, too, because school pictures were the next day.

Undeterred, my sisters uttered three words foreshadowing a scene from a horror movie.

"Let's fix it."

My cut went from bad to worse. They used bigger rollers and a blowout kit dryer. By the time they were finished, I looked like I had stuck my hand in an electrical outlet.

Fortunately, time heals all bad hair experiments. Years later, when finger waves were on the menu, a neighbor used a hot pressing and crimping wave iron to give me a smooth, wavy look. Besides burning off the front of my hair, it turned out okay—by the fifth time she tried it.

I liked cool hair styles because they got me attention from girls. But there was a downside. The hair products made my scalp itch like crazy and it was a challenge not to scratch. Cool hair also kept me from playing sports because I couldn't allow a great hairstyle to get ruined by a bunch of sweat.

I had a smile on my face, remembering those days as I walked through the mall in search of Momma's purple pantyhose. When I spotted a barbershop, I remembered one instance shortly after moving in with Calvin and Momma, when I went to the barbershop on my own with a fresh crisp dollar bill from Calvin's drawer.

Calvin and I spent lots of time together, tinkering in the garage, and I looked up to him a great deal, but when it came to physical appearance, I always admired Momma's classy style, and on that day, I was determined to make her proud of me.

Outside of the Baptist Church and a Black Panther rally, the barbershop was about the Blackest place on the planet, but I didn't know that at the time.

"My momma said give me a haircut," I said, "and my sister said to be sure to give me a light-skinned soul brother look."

The place went silent. Two barbers looked at each other.

"Nigga, don't look at me, you know I can't cut that straight stuff!"

An older gentleman, who I figured was the owner, approached one of the barbers.

"Wasn't you in the Army and didn't you cut hair in Vietnam?"

"Man, you know it was segregated out there. Besides, they sure didn't let no brothers cut no White folks' hair."

I sat down while they tried to figure this out. They flipped through the television channels and found inspiration from *The Little Rascals*. When Alfalfa appeared with his cowlick, the owner told the barber to copy his haircut. I popped down in the styling chair and gave the man the one-dollar bill. He told me it cost two dollars and I assured him that I would come back with my mother with the other dollar.

As soon as she saw what they had done to me, she unleashed the thunder and lightning. She was already irritated because her hair was wet. Black women have a love-hate relationship with rain. They love to hate the rain because it messes up their hair.

Despite the pouring rain, Momma dragged me back to the barber shop without realizing I was not under the umbrella for most of the three-block trek. By the time we got there, I looked like a dripping wet dog and the only evidence that remained of my horrific cut was a stubborn cowlick sticking out in the back.

That day, I was introduced to the "Blackest" side of Lemell Studevent. She shook the umbrella, screamed at me for being so wet, and stormed into the shop.

"Who in the hell cut my son's hair? Is it true that you were looking at *The Little Rascals* as a guide, fool?"

Everyone was bewildered because Momma had just declared that I was her son.

"Oh! Oh! I get this, y'all niggas was excited when he said he was coming back with his Momma to pay that other dollar. Thought a White girl was coming in here, didn't you?"

She looked at me.

"Raymond, which one of these niggas messed your hair up?"

I felt so empowered in that moment that I dropped an N-bomb! I wiped my wet hand on my pant leg and pointed my finger at the guy who cut my hair, who happened to be the owner.

"It was that big-nosed nigga' right there, Momma, him with the glasses."

She chuckled for a second before resuming her verbal beatdown.

"Look, big nose, how can you cut hair that bad? Fool, you got glasses on!"

After some customers laughed, she started "undressing" each of the barbers.

"What are you laughing at fat boy? Is this skinny chic your woman? Makes sense, together y'all look like the number 10. She's the one and you're the zero."

She moved on to the next barber.

"I know you ain't laughin' big lips. You used to come to the library and try to read. But you couldn't see the pages because your lips are too big. You don't need an umbrella in this rain. Just pull that bottom lip over your head and you can cover your whole body, and fat boy can fit under it, too!"

Even a couple of patrons who thought it was funny, mistakenly thought they were exempt from Momma's onslaught of insults. She turned and faced a really dark-skinned fellow in his twenties.

"And you too, Charcoal! You can't get a haircut! You're so Black he can't even see your hairline. I thought I smelled smoke or burning hair when I walked in. That was your Black behind, so Black you smell like smoke!"

His friend laughed so she went after him.

"And, your buddy, wow, how can you have nappy eyebrows! Tilt your head back and I bet your nose hairs are nappy as well!"

By that time, the shop was in an uproar, reminiscent of a comedy club. Then the owner interrupted Momma and made the mistake of asking her for the dollar I owed.

"Nigga, have you lost your mind! You better give me my money back! *The Little Rascals*! Your Afro looks like Buckwheat, so what else would I expect? Where did you learn to cut hair?"

"I was cutting hair in 'Nam."

"You were in 'Nam? Hmm, no wonder we're losing the war. Come on Raymond, let's go."

As we walked out the door, I pumped my fist in a Black Power gesture.

"Right on, brothers," I said, as I stuck out my tongue at the guy who ruined my hair.

"BUCKWHEAT!"

In Black culture, a game known as "Playing the Dozens" consists of participants creatively making fun of one another by talking about his or her mother. It is thought to have originated in New Orleans during the slave trade. According to legend, the lowest of the slaves were gathered in groups of dozens, hence "the lowest dozen" or the bottom of the pile. It still exists. I was officially introduced to it that day at the Benning Road Barber Shop when Lemell crushed those guys and made it feel more like "Playing the Hundreds!"

I loved how Momma defended me as well as Calvin ever had. I felt her love when she held my hand the entire time. It was as if she didn't want me to get nervous. But what I remember most was the brief exchange we had on the walk home.

"Way to get 'em Momma. Can you teach me how to talk bad about people like that?"

"I sure can, but only if you promise me something."

She stopped, leaned down to my eye level and for the first and only time I can recall, she grabbed me softly by the chin.

"Raymond, listen closely. I know you enjoyed watching me give it to those guys back there. But if you want me to teach you how to talk about folks' and their ugly mommas, you have to promise me not to use the word 'nigga' ever again, especially outside the house. It's not a good word and I need you to keep it off that li'l sassy tongue of yours. People may be offended a bit more when you say it."

I was bewildered by what she had said.

"But everybody uses it, and me and my friends call each other 'nigga' all the time. They don't seem to mind."

"That's because they know your family."

"Oh, so because they know my family is all niggas."

She squeezed my chin firmly.

"Raymond, don't use that word, ever, and I mean ever! We may refer to ourselves that way sometimes, but never think that you, me, and any Black person you ever see is a 'nigga.'"

That conversation stayed relevant for the rest of my life. It wasn't far from my mind as I shopped for Momma's pantyhose. I finally found the right color, but just to be sure, I bought every pair on the shelf so Momma would never have to worry about having purple pantyhose again. I even bought her a pair of matching authentic Gucci shoes so her feet wouldn't hurt.

When I got back to her room, I knocked softly, but she didn't answer. I slowly opened the door and tiptoed inside. She wasn't napping. She was on her knees, praying.

"Lord, I can't stay and pray long because these knees are getting old. I'm in my fifties now and I just want to thank you for all these years. I know my memory is failing me so I cannot remember all the blessings you have given me. Lord, I suppose you have a sense of humor and maybe you sent that young fella' here to amuse me. I just want to ask that you help me with my memory because I am forgetting so many things. Please, help the young man who is obviously one of your lost sheep. He doesn't know who his family is so please help him find them and help me be nice and kind to the White guy. I know I shouldn't call him White, but you know my struggles with loving those folks. Please forgive me and help him find my purple pantyhose so I can look good for you in church today. Please help me with my memory because I am forgetting so many things. Amen."

She thanked the Lord for her fifty years of life. Obviously, Momma had no idea how old she really was, and fifty was long in the rearview mirror. The last thing I heard her pray for was the purple pantyhose.

"Your prayers have been answered," I said, when I was sure she was finished.

I handed her the packages of hose and then the authentic Gucci pumps. She was elated and broke into a revised rendition of the 23rd Psalm.

"The Lord is my shepherd, and although I walk through the valley of death I will not fall because he done blessed me with a pair of Gucci, *woochie* babies! Shucks, even that crazy fool Prince ain't got no purple *this* color!"

Knowing she felt grateful, I figured she would at least allow me to share the "Greaster Sunday" story. She agreed and enjoyed it, but just as I finished, her caregiver walked in and announced that visiting time was over. I assured Momma that I would be back the next day.

"Promise to come by as early as possible, because you are a great storyteller. Did you work for Sesame Street or Walt Disney?"

She laughed and looked at the nurse.

"You folks need to hire this guy to entertain the residents with his storytelling. His imagination is incredible. Who you going to be tomorrow, my former White professor at Howard University who taught African-American studies? On second thought, maybe come a little late, and I'll believe you are my son because Black folks are always late. And by the way, don't bite your nails! That's a nasty habit!"

7

"This is Mississippi alright. Even the state flower is white."

I asked to borrow a pillow and blanket so I could spend the night in the Cadillac, parked in the rear lot. From there, I'd have a good view of Momma's room. I sat there for a while, just breathing in deeply and exhaling. I felt like a complete train wreck. A quick glance in the mirror confirmed that I was a mess—physically and emotionally.

Just as my tummy began to growl, I spotted a Popeye's Chicken across the street. I headed straight to the drive-up window and ordered a four-piece meal with a large sweet tea. Gentrification in DC? Hmm, if eating fried chicken while sitting in a Cadillac on the rugged southeast side of Chocolate City isn't a classic example of it then I don't know what is. Actually, to borrow Momma's word, it's just about as "Niggafied" as it can get.

My Cadillac rental sure didn't smell like a "lac," as we used to say. Calvin's Caddy always smelled like Brut cologne while Momma's had the aroma of leather with a tinge of cigarette smoke. She loved the signature cardboard scent trees and kept one dangling from the rearview mirror like most cars in the neighborhood.

"If you look good and smell good," she'd say, "then you feel good."

I am six foot, three, so sleeping in a car has never been comfortable for me. In this case, it didn't matter because what was going on with Momma weighed heavy on my mind. I caught a glimpse of the Mississippi Avenue street sign and began to reminisce about the influence the state of Mississippi had on my life and even more on Momma's. Our first trip to Crystal Springs, Mississippi in 1973 left an indelible impression on me and I never looked at Momma, life or racism the same again. There isn't any other state in the union that conjures up more emotions within the Black community than Mississippi. The "M-word" is not far behind the "N-word" as far as some Black folks are concerned. Over the next twelve months, the Magnolia State would play a major role in all of our lives.

For what seemed like hours, cramped in the backseat of the Cadillac, I wondered if I should dare bring up the word Mississippi to Momma. Should I take the risk of upsetting her? Would the dark tales of Mississippi jolt her memory and trigger her to recall something suppressed within the deepest cavern of her mind?

You could assume that the traumatic events of growing up in the segregated South were enough to make me not want to bring up the name to her. Sadly, it was the events that happened over the span of a few months while she was in her forties that cast a shadow much darker than any Jim Crow nonsense or from what the Grand Wizard of the Klan could cause. In fact, the word Mississippi was almost never mentioned in the Studevent household.

I was afraid to talk about it. I believe it represented such a dark place in my life as well, and I was not cool about opening the door to those emotions. Before deciding if I could lay any of that out for Momma, I rewound the tape in my mind to see if I was able to handle the emotions I had suppressed as a result of the "dark days of Mississippi."

Even though Momma and I had shared some tender moments, she still held back from fully embracing me. She remained a mystery because I could never figure her feelings. She wasn't moody, but I never knew when it was safe to tease her or try to make her laugh.

Once I realized she had a sense of humor, I figured that was my inroad to her heart. Sometimes, when I was given a chore to do, I would talk like a slave to get her to laugh.

"I sho'iz a good Negro, wantin' ta please ya ma, I be a good li'l white Negro Masa Ma'am."

Obviously, I had no idea how deep my silly gestures cut her to the core. I used to sing or hum Negro spirituals as well. Calvin and the girls would laugh.

"I know you want to laugh, too, Momma."

I learned later that slavery goofs were not acceptable any longer and it quickly became clear why slavery jokes were so sensitive. At times, I felt as if Momma wanted to make sure she didn't get too close to me because she knew it was wrong to take out her disdain for White folks on an innocent child. She always provided for me materially, but I still felt a protective wall she worked hard to build between us. I saw it when she cut off her laugh midway through, almost to keep herself from liking me or getting used to having me around.

Time would reveal that Mississippi was the problem.

She dealt with a number of issues that were foreign to me. Calvin was light-skinned and so were his siblings. Most of his sisters did not take too kindly to their older brother marrying a brown-skinned woman, from Mississippi no less. She never felt comfortable around her in-laws.

Although she had a terrible childhood, she got so excited talking to her relatives there.

Momma's brother called to say that their father was not doing well, and she should come see him before he passed. We were going to the place I had heard so much about and I was finally going to meet the relatives with the funny accents.

I had no idea that Mississippi was 900 miles from DC. We had to leave at night in order to arrive in Birmingham, Alabama at the break of dawn before continuing on to Mississippi. Black folks could not be caught driving during the night in Alabama or Mississippi. On top of that, we were a Black family in a Cadillac with Washington, DC, tags, with a "kidnapped" White child in the car.

We stopped for gas in Virginia, which Momma said was not the "real South." During that pit stop she was emphatic about two things.

"First, be sure to use the restroom and second, nobody drink anything. I want all your bladders completely empty, including you Calvin."

Her reasoning was simple. We could not stop for a bathroom break and risk being spotted by any White folks in Tennessee, Alabama or Mississippi.

Calvin and Lemell argued more on that trip than the entire time I had known them! They never really argued, but rather agreed to disagree. Besides, Calvin wanted no part of dealing with Lemell's wit. She had not been in Mississippi for a long time, so her memory was based on the years of segregation. She didn't care about the Civil Rights Act and all of the legislation adopted in the sixties. She felt that White people down there would be even worse than they were then because they were told to embrace segregation.

According to her account years later, most of the arguments

centered around Calvin underestimating the hatred some folks in the South felt toward Black folks.

"Calvin, you're driving too fast!"

"Baby, I'm doing the speed limit."

"I don't care. Go slow because I don't want to get to Alabama too fast and it's still dark."

"What are you looking at, Baby? I know that is not a *Green Book*! Honey this is 1973, we don't need that."

"As long as you keep humping the road at this speed we will have to check into a Negro Only hotel."

Things went from bad to worse.

"Momma!" Cookie said, "Scoop keeps farting and it stinks!"

"Momma, I have to do number two really bad."

"Lord have mercy! Calvin, where are we?"

"We are at the Virginia and Tennessee state line, so we are safe."

"Safe! Safe? Darling, they got Klan all over this area. You want to know how I know? Because for the past 100 miles I ain't seen one Negro. Translation, Klanville."

"You mean Knoxville."

"No, Klanville, and in case you forgot, what city did we just drive through?"

"Lynchburg."

"I rest my case, Negro."

Momma proceeded to give her hubby some more Southern roasting and food for thought.

"Calvin, White folks got code words that colored folks down here understand. They mean none of us are allowed. Here is your first lesson, so listen up kids. You ain't never heard about no Black folks living in any place with a 'Ville in the name. Think about *it*.

Knoxville? White folks. A place in Virginia called Danville. You really think Negroes are allowed to live in a place called Danville? Psst, sound about as white as lettuce. Look, we are about to drive pass another Ville in the morning in Alabama. Huntsville. Did you hear me, Sweetheart? I said Hunts-ville. What do you think they hunting? Calvin, trust me; them White folks ain't hunting rabbits. Oh, they got one that sounds Black, yeah; they tried to fool us with Jacksonville. Jackson...that's about as Black a name as you can find. Trying to fool us into thinking it's some of us there."

Momma laughed and put her head in *The Green Book*.

"Your move."

"Baby, I know a *Ville* where it's all negroes."

"Where?"

Calvin laughed.

"Coupe de Ville, as in this Cadillac Coupe de Ville we're sitting in. There's all Negroes in here."

Cookie laughed and looked at me.

"Well, almost all negroes."

We were rolling along but Calvin had to address my poop situation immediately.

"Unfasten your pants and start pushing and when you're ready for it to fall, let me know."

I pushed and yelled as if I were in a maternity ward.

"I'm ready Daddy!"

He pulled over with a screech. I jumped out in the darkest night I had ever seen. Unable to see absolutely anything, I pooped, wiped and jumped back in the car.

The following morning, I saw the sign I had been waiting to see.

"Welcome to Mississippi, The Magnolia State."

"This is Mississippi alright," said Momma. "Even the state flower is white."

She got eerily quiet the closer we got to Jackson. Then I saw a sign that I could not believe: Jackson 20 miles. Raymond 34 miles. That was the first time I had seen my name on a sign. Momma was not amused, and I soon found out why she wasn't too fond of the city of Raymond.

We finally turned onto a long dusty driveway. These were common to avoid road noise, but they also allowed time for a family to prepare for the police or Klan members.

I saw three small houses a few yards apart. The family gave us a warm country welcome. I followed Cookie and Linda's lead and greeted them accordingly.

The pink elephant in the room was my complexion and how I was related to these Negroes. The children greeted me as if they had known me for years. Despite all the racial animus, these folks seemed happier than "free" Negroes I had ever been around in DC.

Momma's mother, affectionately referred to as "Big Momma," was completely blind. She asked to get a hug from her new grandbaby, Raymond, but when she felt my hair, she was bewildered. It didn't take her long to realize that it was straight and had a different texture. She didn't waste any time asking about my parents.

"Mell is my Momma," I said proudly, "and Calvin is my Daddy."

"Mell, I didn't even know you was pregnant!" Big Momma said. "Calvin, you must be part Indian like me, for that boy to have straight hair like that."

While the boys, Andy and Fat Pat were warm and kind, I could not help but notice my two new gorgeous cousins: Sharon, known as Danny and her sister Magnolia, known as Mac. They were five

and six years older than me but who cared? Aunt Connie was probably twenty-five years older than me and it didn't matter in the least.
True love is true love. The sad part was, I knew I was going to have
to tell Aunt Connie that she was no longer my main crush. Mac was
a younger version of her and Danny was just lighter. Danny seemed
wild and crazy but Mac was so beautiful and had me smitten before
the Cadillac had time to cool off. Nowadays, she is known in Jackson as Maggie Wade, the anchor on NBC-WLBT Channel 3 News.
Everyone thought it was so cute that I kept asking, "Where's Mac?"

Momma was tickled and seemed to be having a wonderful time.

"Boy, stop staring at that girl," she kept telling me.

"Well, at least he likes Black girls and he's not thinking he's White
and wanted to get himself a Becky Sue."

Calvin joined the men in manly stuff. I discovered years later that
they were talking about two football players at Jackson State University: Walter Payton and Jackie Slater. Both local heroes went on to
have Hall of Fame careers in the NFL.

Some of the men were arguing whether there would be riots the
following baseball season after Hank Aaron broke Babe Ruth's home
run record.

"Imagine that, brothers," said Calvin, "a Black man will own the
most hallowed record in all of American sports. The home run king!"

Lemell stopped dead in her tracks and uttered what would become
the quote of the summer. "I keep telling you Black folks that Babe
Ruth was Black. I saw three pictures of him in a new magazine at
the library. In one, he's wearing a mink coat, second, he's playing the
saxophone, and, finally, his nose is wider than all of ours. Mink coat,
saxophone, and a bell-pepper nose . . . Negro!"

We all laughed. As we headed to the market to get some candy, I
asked momma if she wanted anything.

"Yeah, get me a Baby Ruth chocolate bar!"

Mac, Danny and Cookie bonded while I befriended the boys. I was fascinated with the chickens, pigs and other farm animals. It felt so different running through the fields. I am tempted to say that I felt so free, but it's hard to use that word when referring to anything in Mississippi. We ate lots of food and then I got to meet the real character of the family, Big Daddy. He loved to drink and laugh, which exposed the reddish hue of his skin. He and Big Momma were part Indian.

For the next few days, it was great seeing Momma have a wonderful time with her family. Even at a young age, I could tell she was glad to be around her own folks.

Of course, I learned that Mississippi is not always fun and I found out why the city of Raymond was a problem for Momma. Her father took the family to the place in Raymond where a cousin had been hung from a tree.

"My cousin, George Robinson, was lynched right here. I remember the day because Lemell you were only a few months old. It was August 15, 1930, and you were born in April that year. We had a lot of our folks strung up back then."

We could still see rope marks on the branches. The moment Momma looked into my blue eyes, she seemed to have flashbacks of the Klansmen with their piercing blue eyes staring at her from behind their hoods.

"I heard them call you Scoop," Big Daddy said. "I hate the name Raymond, so is it alright if we call you Scoop?"

"I hate the name Raymond too."

"Why?"

"Because it's my real father's name and he left me. Calvin is my real father."

Even at that age, I realized that the racial conflict in Mississippi could not be taken lightly, because it could cost someone their life.

While driving back, or should I say, "While driving Black," Big Daddy, Andy, Pat and I were pulled over by a state trooper. When the officer opened the back door of our car, he saw me sitting between a row of Black kids and made the snap judgment that I had been kidnapped.

"Are you sure you're okay, boy?"

I assured him I was fine. The boys froze as if he might kill us all.

"You been drinking, Boy?"

I was bewildered that he was referring to Big Daddy as "Boy." Mississippi was quickly living up to its reputation. The trooper kept his shades on so I couldn't see his eyes, but I imagined them as blue as the ocean. He snooped around some more and when he got tired of exerting his authority and trying to intimidate Big Daddy, he sent us on our way.

When we rejoined the family, I blended right in by performing one of the dances that Cookie had taught me while watching *Soul Train*. Then I heard a police siren, which triggered a post-traumatic stress reaction deeply buried in my psyche, and I took off running and screaming. Two Mississippi State Trooper vehicles had arrived to investigate why a White child was on a Black family's property. The trooper who stopped us earlier had alerted his partners, and they assumed something was wrong when I took off running. They pulled their guns, spit out some racial slurs and made hostile demands while threatening to shoot "any nigger that moves."

When Momma tried to comfort me, the trooper intercepted her, slammed her to the ground, pushed his boot against her neck and handcuffed her. I screaming at the officers.

"Get your hands off my Momma!"

Fortunately, Momma's brother, Nelson, had done some work in town for one of the trooper's family. He quickly stepped in front of Calvin to address the trooper.

"Officer Shinley…"

"I don't believe I heard you address me properly, boy."

Nelson quickly corrected himself.

"I mean Officer Shinley, Sir! My sister Mell here takin' good care of some really fine White folk up round' Virginia countryside. They wanted some time on a boat cruise and so they kindly as' my sis here, Miss Mell, to take good care of dey fine young lad Raymond. And, Sir, he real smart and like a lil' genius down here for us Negroes, helping us understand how smart White folk is. He so smart…uh, Sir."

The trooper looked at me and asked if that was true. Suspecting that I was about to say something that might get us all into trouble, Momma squeezed my hand really tight.

"Yes, sir."

I couldn't believe I was looking at the scariest blue eyes I had ever seen. They were cold, emotionless and filled with pure evil. That was my first real lesson in Southern bigotry and that these White folks don't mess around. All the men restrained Calvin and took him for a walk through the pasture to cool him off.

To see a policeman throw Momma to the ground and reduce her to nothing but a rag doll made it all clear. Momma knew that these White men would not hesitate to shoot her, dead like a dog. I thought of all her warnings while we drove to Mississippi. Calvin was made a believer, too. I was so sad that a grown woman of forty-three was treated no different than she was at the age of ten. This was 1973. Unbelievable.

I didn't know what to think, let alone say. I wanted to be close to her and tell her that I was sorry about those mean White folks. One night, Momma and I were sitting on the porch with Big Momma, waiting for her to fall asleep. After she walked her mother to her bed, I started crying and gave Momma a hug.

"I am sorry you had to deal with this place."

She hugged me and said nothing. The rest of our time was uneventful and I'm ashamed to admit that the magnitude of what I experienced in Mississippi faded rather quickly

The Mississippi Avenue street sign brought back these memories and gave me an idea. If Momma saw the name, it might jump-start her memory. I went to the facility administrator, explained my idea and asked permission to take Momma outside for a walk. It was a risk, and I didn't want to upset her, but I was convinced that she could come out of this fog.

Momma had too much wit left in her for me to quit. She probably didn't know Mississippi Avenue from the Mississippi River, let alone the state of Mississippi. But there had to be some nerve endings in her brain that still held some memories. The hardest task would be convincing her to take a walk with me outside.

One of Momma's nurses opened the door while I stood back a few steps.

"That White man is back again! I told him that I don't know him. Ain't no honkies in my family. Besides, he's wearing the same clothes he had on yesterday. He's just a dirty White boy living out his White guilt trip or something. No child of mine would wear the same clothes two days in a row. Same funky drawers and socks on. Boy, go take a shower!"

I knew she was going to be tough on me, but I didn't expect her to spew out such venom. The nurse must have sensed how hopeless I was feeling, and Momma likely wouldn't have stepped into the hallway with me, let alone the street, so the nurse agreed to accompany us outside. Even this was a struggle, but Momma finally caved in.

"I'll go, but I don't want the dirty White boy to touch me!"

As we neared the Mississippi Avenue sign, I stopped and said the word with a down-home redneck accent.

"Mississippi, Mississippi!"

I looked at Momma, waiting for a reaction or a comment about my blue eyes. She picked up her walker and slammed it into the concrete. Her eyes never left mine, and I honestly don't even think she blinked the whole time.

Suddenly, she bowed her head and began to pray out loud, but I could tell she was on the verge of losing control of her emotions.

"Get away from me! Get away from me!"

The nurse tried to calm her down by softly rubbing her shoulders.

"Lady, get your hands off me! Will you both leave me be for a bit, please?"

We stepped away as she stared intensely at the sign. I didn't enjoy seeing her tormented by demons from her past, but I hoped it would trigger memories about who I was. Her eyes stayed glued to the sign for a long time as we just stood there. She slowly bowed her head, and I caught a glimpse of a tear roll down her cheek, under her eyeglasses, and off the tip of her nose.

I took a few steps toward her.

"I'm so sorry, Momma. I'm so sorry."

She pivoted in her house slippers and held onto her walker.

"Young man, I have no idea who you are, what you want, or why the hell you keep coming here and getting my blood pressure up. Now, if you and this fine young lady would be so kind as to walk me back to my place and allow me to rest 'til lunch, I'd be much obliged."

Feeling dejected, we walked Momma back to her room. I told her that I had taken a two-week vacation and was going back to California before I lost my job, but I promised to visit her once a month. Once again, she accused me of being a liar.

"I have never lied to you about anything, Momma."

"You lied about that being your Cadillac."

"Why do you say that?"

"First, there's no front license plate on a real Cadillac and second, I saw the rental car key tag. Now let me go to sleep, young man. See you next month. Maybe then you will have a Mercedes-Benz and tell me that you're the president of the United States. Close my door, please, and go take a shower. You stink, young man. You smell like fried chicken."

I tried to process what had just transpired. Maybe I was delusional, but I was convinced that seeing the street sign made a crack in her armor and it gave me a glimmer of hope. I needed to fly home and regroup, then do a major Google search to uncover every gigabyte of available information on how to fool that evil bastard, "Mr. Alzheimer."

Maybe for my next visit, I'd rent a Mercedes. See if she remembered the Cadillac. Who was I kidding? She was more likely to remember the lie I told her. We would see next month. Meanwhile, I had my own memories of Mississippi to put to rest.

8

"I am going to raise you as my own."

Based on the last conversation I had with Momma, I figured I'd better live up to her expectations so I reserved a Mercedes-Benz for my next trip. Not responding to her surly quips could easily be construed as disrespectful in her eyes and might prompt her to suggest that I was a spineless sissy, certainly not someone she raised. Since my boss's mother had recently died from Alzheimer's, he gave me the green light to take a few days off each month. My first move would be to park a Mercedes right outside her window, with the rental tags removed for good measure.

The importance I put on winning petty battles with Momma reminded me of just how strained and even competitive our relationship had always been. The stakes were much higher now as we fought a common foe in Alzheimer's. I wondered if she had any idea of how devastating this disease is, but I was pretty sure she would find a way to blame the evil White man and twist my arm into being her spokesperson.

"Yes, Mr. Alzheimer was surely a White man," I'd say, "who created the disease out of spite to kill off Black folks, like they did to them brothers down in Tuskegee, Alabama."

I was determined to bring something positive into her life to get her to remember me. While my rational side knew this was unrealistic, my love for Momma made me Google "remarkable Alzheimer's recoveries," which led to hopeful stories that gave me a glimmer of hope. One way or the other, I was looking for Momma to validate my existence.

When we moved her into the facility, I took many of Calvin's medals and awards for safekeeping. He was incredibly accomplished, a highly decorated Marine and a revered Mason. Few things in life made Momma prouder than his accomplishments in the United States Marine Corps. She bragged to everyone how they lived in Japan, San Diego and San Francisco and that Calvin fought bravely in the Korean War and in Vietnam. If the Mississippi Street sign could conjure up emotion in Momma than Calvin's military memorabilia might resonate, too.

Selecting which of Calvin's memorabilia I should take with me stirred up many memories of my childhood with him. He created such a warm and loving environment for our family. Calvin was the father I needed—my savior and role model for how a man should behave. He was the most charismatic and inspirational man I had ever known, and his loss was crushing.

Every Friday afternoon, I sat by the window, waiting for Calvin to arrive from work. As soon as I caught a glimpse of the Cadillac, and the blinker signaling the turn off Minnesota Avenue, I tried to beat him to the back door so that when that big ole' land yacht slowly crept near the driveway, I'd be in position, standing at attention like a good cadet.

Calvin would stop short of the driveway and signal his little buck private to the car.

"Okay Private Scoop, take us home."

Sitting on his lap with my big blue eyes wide open, I'd steer the gold Cadillac into the driveway.

"Mission accomplished, Sergeant Daddy!"

I could smell the fresh catfish Calvin had brought home. I always looked forward to chopping off the heads and gutting them. Once clean, we'd dip them in cornmeal and toss them into a deep pan of spattering hot grease. Cookie and I fought to sit on Calvin's lap and be his favorite child of the evening. He was so big and loving. He allowed both of us to sit on one leg.

He picked through my fish to make sure I didn't choke on a bone. I remember thinking, that these Black folks could sure fry fish and chicken, but both were a little scary to eat because you could choke to death if a bone got caught in your throat.

There was always a loaf of bread on the table, ready to coax a lodged bone down somebody's throat. They always told a Southern tale about a cousin who died from choking on a bone. That said, the deep-fried catfish and fried chicken were so good it was worth the risk.

Truth be told, I think the grease and the mandatory hot sauce drove up a lot of Black folks' blood pressure and killed far more than any bones ever did.

Whenever I smell fried fish, that aroma takes back to those Friday nights. These memories always make me smile, even if they're bittersweet.

As I prepared for round one of my monthly battle with Momma and Mr. Alzheimer, I pulled out Calvin's Mason ring, which was huge and heavy because his hands were so big. As a child, I found it mysterious and magical. It had a weird symbol with the letter G engraved in the center. I didn't know what it stood for, but since Calvin was the coolest dude I had ever known, it had to be something special.

Just holding the ring now on a Friday afternoon made me feel surrounded by his presence and hopeful that it could resurrect Momma's memories about Calvin and the rest of us.

Most of our family photos had been destroyed in a flood many years ago. I begged Cookie and Linda to find some pictures or get some from family in Mississippi. To my surprise, my sisters had a few pictures that survived the disaster. They thought Momma was too far gone to look at old photos, and according to the doctors, she was rapidly approaching stage six of Alzheimer's, also known as middle dementia, a period of severe cognitive decline, when a person has scant memory of recent events and forgets the names of close friends or family. Linda and Cookie had already showed her photos with no success and felt that she would just get upset if I tried the same thing.

Maybe, I was in self-denial, but I had read about a case of miraculous memory return. With every piece of memorabilia I found, my memory got stronger yet Momma couldn't remember her own children. Talk about a cruel joke life can play on you.

I found a picture of me and Calvin with my first bicycle on the day I proved to the neighborhood that I no longer needed training wheels. We installed a horn on the bike and cut straws to put in the wheel spokes. Other than respecting the elders in the house, nothing seemed more important to Black folks than looking good. My bike was no different, and Calvin made sure it was the Cadillac of two-wheeled vehicles.

I came across a photo from church, where Calvin and I were dressed alike in matching, pinstriped three-piece suits. We looked so sharp we could have been headlining The Cotton Club. I prayed that this picture would make Momma's heart skip a beat because Calvin looked so handsome. For as long as I'd known her, Momma never hesitated to acknowledge a good-looking Black man when she saw one.

But nothing excited Momma more than seeing a Marine in his dress blues. The picture of Calvin was sure to cause a breakthrough or a bust. I felt confident that even if she didn't remember her own husband; she would claim him anyway.

Calvin had a fascination with guns and was holding one in nearly all of the pictures from his Marine days. When I was seven, he bought me a BB gun rifle and told me I was going to be the "B.B. King" of the neighborhood. I had no idea who he was, but Calvin loved him and that was good enough for me.

While I had seen the tough streets of DC, I hadn't yet become a victim of its violence. That changed in the blink of an eye once I ventured outside the house. My days as cute curly-haired Scoop were over. I became the "pretty boy" of the neighborhood who the hardened kids feasted on at every imaginable turn. My indoctrination was swift, brutal, and violent. One day, I was in the driveway, holding my BB gun, when a big kid from the local housing project walked up and punched me in the face.

"Give me your gun, White boy!"

He snatched it, walked off laughing, and called me a sissy.

Calvin heard the ruckus and came out in a flash. At 240 pounds, he was a formidable presence. He took off running, snatched the kid by the collar and dragged him back to where I was standing, still stunned from the unexpected fist.

"Raymond, punch this boy right in his face the same way he punched you. I mean it, Raymond, now!"

I stood in shock because I had never seen Calvin that mad, and he had never called me Raymond before. I was more scared of him than that kid, so I hauled off and hit that boy directly in his mouth. Calvin threw the boy down and pointed the BB gun at him.

"The next time you touch my son, I'm going to shoot you right in your face. And you tell all the boys in the projects that if the little White kid on the corner has any problems with any of you, the baddest man in DC is coming for them!"

Calvin asked me if I was alright and gave me a lesson.

"If I ever hear that you ran away from standing up for yourself, you will have to deal with me. I would be disappointed if you shamed the Studevent name by being labeled a punk."

I realized I needed to learn how to fight. That lesson served me well throughout my life.

Calvin asked me how it felt to get revenge.

"It felt good to punch him in his mouth."

"Always punch first," he said. "Ask questions later."

Another valuable lesson for surviving the streets of DC.

The final picture I discovered of Calvin was my favorite. He is in front of my old elementary school, sitting in The Bookmobile. When he came to my school, it was the greatest feeling ever and I bragged to all my friends that my father was the driver. They didn't believe me until Calvin hugged me in front of hundreds of children.

This public display of affection made me feel so special. I had a father, and I called him the most important word a young boy learns to say: "Daddy."

I woke up from a nap and immediately resumed assembling my official Calvin Studevent biography package, hoping that Momma might recognize vital figures from her past. As I did, I thought back to the most traumatic week of my life.

While Calvin had created a wonderful family environment, Momma and I settle in. I started to feel as though she was thinking of me as a permanent fixture in the house. Although the official adoption papers had not yet been signed, the situation felt permanent. I had finally found peace and love in an environment most kids in DC dream of and never realize.

Momma would occasionally scold me because she sensed that Calvin had a soft spot for me. Sometimes, I got in trouble for trying to fit in with the older boys. We would do silly things, like letting the air out of neighbors' tires or tying a bunch of soda cans to the back of cars so when they drove down the street they made a ruckus of noise. One of my favorite pranks was putting a rock inside each hubcap and the driver couldn't figure out what was causing the noise. Some kids would go to three different pay phones, dial 911 and send the police or fire trucks to an annoying neighbor's house. I was too scared to do that then, but I made up for it later in life.

Momma and Calvin had a loving and nurturing marriage. They cooked together, went dancing on the weekends, and always showed tremendous respect for one another. They were a fine example of what a marriage should be. Lemell really loved Calvin and he was absolutely in love with her.

In the summer of 1974, Lemell flew down to Mississippi ahead of us because her brother, David, had died. Calvin and us kids joined her in time for the funeral. Being so young, the sight of a dead body in a casket really affected me, not to mention the sight of people falling all over the body and carrying on. To see David's children and wife come apart like that was impossible to relate to at such a young age.

I couldn't understand why everyone kept saying he was in a "better place in heaven," while they seemed to be coming unglued. I was about to find out exactly what they were feeling.

Calvin and Momma decided to stay a while longer, in spite of an extreme heat wave. The air was so heavy you could hardly breathe.

"Boy it's hot out here today," said Calvin. "You kids better drink plenty of water."

As he stepped onto the front porch, he began rubbing his head, looking distressed. A few moments later, he collapsed right in front of me, hitting the ground hard. I went numb with shock. What just happened? Was he joking? Everyone began screaming and rushing to his aid. Uncles and cousins picked him up and laid him in the backseat of Uncle Ed's car. After Mell jumped in, they hit the gravel road at a hundred miles an hour. The black Oldsmobile streaked into the distance, kicking up a cloud of smoke in its wake. I had an uneasy feeling in the pit of my stomach. The house was eerily silent for the rest of the day as we prayed and waited for news from the hospital. The day passed into night as we all collapsed into a fitful sleep.

The next day, Momma had still not returned from the hospital and there was no word on Calvin's condition. I walked around in circles, praying to God, begging him not to take away the only man who had ever meant something to me. Then I saw Momma walk into the house. When the phone rang, I made a mad dash to see who had called. Everyone was quiet, and I asked if Daddy was going to be alright. Nobody said a word. They all just dropped their heads.

"Momma, is Daddy okay? Momma? Momma! I've been praying to that God you been telling me is so good. Tell me Momma, did God take my Daddy away?"

She didn't say a word. I knew what that meant. I screamed, from deep within my soul. I kept screaming as I ran into the fields in back of the house, going as fast and far as I could before I collapsed to the ground.

"*Noooooo*! God, I begged you not to take him away! God, you don't care about watching little kids cry in pain. You don't care that my new family has no father. God, you don't care! You took away the only person who ever loved me! You don't care!"

I heard people calling out from a distance.

"Scoop, Scoop!"

I also detected the muffled sounds of my cousins Andy and Mac, trying to find me. They sat around me as I kept my face in the ground, crying uncontrollably. I recall saying just one thing when I got back to the house.

"Please not one of you talk to me about God, Jesus, and my daddy being in a better place. God would rather watch us all suffer than create a new angel instead of taking my daddy."

I walked outside and eventually fell under a tree by a lake and cried for hours.

Calvin had died of a massive stroke brought on by the sweltering heat and dehydration. He was forty-seven years old. He had hypertension and was overweight. He had been such a proud Marine, so some said it was only fitting that he died on this day—the Fourth of July. Needless to say, ever since then, the holiday has taken on a different meaning for me.

Momma was devastated. She had to call Calvin's brother, Uncle Robert, to come and drive us home because she was too distraught to get behind the wheel. The Marine Corp flew his body back to Washington. I don't think we said more than five words on the fourteen-hour drive. All we did was cry. Within a week, Lemell had lost her brother and husband. I remember thinking that's it's over. Calvin was dead and I would never see him again. The man I thought invincible was gone.

During the funeral activities, I stared into the casket at Calvin's uniform and face. Seeing my uncles and aunts wailing away during the funeral distracted me from the fact that he was gone. I couldn't make sense of it. At the cemetery, I was fascinated by the Marine Corps honor guards in their dress blues, systematically firing off the twenty-one-gun salute afforded to those who served their country. That image led me to eventually enroll in a military academy. Momma's face was shrouded by a black veil, as she sat strong and dignified, as usual. When they folded the American flag and handed it to her, she sat up firmly, as if to say, "Calvin, you taught us to be strong, no matter what."

The next day, after all the food was eaten and the out-of-town guests had returned to their respective cities, the house felt eerily quiet. Cookie and Linda were all cried out. Cookie had slammed her bedroom door so hard it nearly tore away from its hinges. While Calvin was my hero, Cookie was a Daddy's girl, and now her father was gone forever. She didn't speak a word for days on end. I would ask her a question, and she would just stare at me blankly, like all the life had gone out of her. Linda wandered around the house and cried. Momma stood firm, undoubtedly because she felt she needed to be strong for us. Now a widow, she would have to put her own grief on hold, put the pieces of our shattered lives together and move ahead, a single mom, responsible for raising three children. What choice did she have?

One of the most pressing issues was what would happen to me. There were no legal papers binding me to her. She could have decided to take me back to my blood relatives, the White folks, and let them take a crack at raising me. One evening, after she spoke with Linda and Cookie about the situation, she called me downstairs.

"Raymond, I know you have been hearing the chatter about what is going to happen to you now that Calvin is gone. Well, you don't have to worry about that any longer. When you saw me whispering to Calvin as he lay in the casket, I made him a promise that I would continue what we started. I am going to raise you as my own. You are now the man of the house. Calvin had big shoes to fill, but now you gotta learn to be a man. He is gone forever."

While I was elated that she was not going to take me back to my White family or God forbid, the orphanage, the fact that my hero was gone had sliced my heart to ribbons. It was a pain that cut right to my core. Those final four words, "he is gone forever," made me scream and run upstairs, where I dove into Calvin's place on their bed and cried uncontrollably for what felt like days. I rubbed at the deep pain in my chest. It was simply too much to endure.

Momma tried in vain to console me. As time went on, I acted out in all kinds of ways. I tested her patience when I refused to go to church, blaspheming God and blaming him for the pain in my life. Momma wanted to chastise me, but she held back. She realized that at the age of seven, I had been forced to deal with too much instability in my life.

I even blamed Calvin.

"Momma, how could he leave us like that? Everything was so good!"

"God called him home, and we have to accept HIS will," she replied.

Her answer only made me angrier.

"So, this God we worship and put money into the collection plate for every week knows how much pain this is causing us? He could have easily created another angel, but instead he decided to take my hero and watch us cry. He also needed your brother two weeks ago. All my life has been nothing but crying, hospitals, and people not wanting me. You can have that God, Momma. Never ask me to step foot back in that church again!"

As if things weren't bad enough, life had another swift kick to give me in my rear end. One extremely hot afternoon while I was sleeping on Calvin's side of the bed, Momma came in, woke me up, and said that my biological mother wanted to talk to me. I leaned over and picked up the phone. Momma shook her head.

"No, she is on the front porch."

I walked outside and saw my mother, looking frail, pale, and like straight-up hell. She handed me a red fire truck.

"Look, it has a hose on it that shoots water. Well, Mommy just came by to say goodbye. I'm a junkie and I can't do anything for you. I'm sorry I can't get off drugs, but I told Lemell to bring me the papers. I'll sign them so she can adopt you. It's what's best for you. Bye, Scoop."

She turned around and got into a waiting taxi. I watched as it disappeared down the street, but she never looked back. That strange, emotionless interaction was the last time I ever saw her. You hear stories about animal mothers who protect their babies from any and all threats, a baked-in instinct, love without boundaries. My mother had no such instinct. The woman who had carried me in her belly for nine months coolly said goodbye without the slightest hint of love, like that cheap plastic truck was supposed to mean something to me.

Both of my biological parents had tossed me aside, valuing me about as much as a dime-store toy. I would occasionally see my name-sake and biological father driving down Minnesota Avenue but he never stopped to say hello to his son.

I sat on the stairs, tears flowing down my cheeks as I spun the wheels on that fire truck as fast as I could, a parting gift from a mother I hardly ever knew.

Momma was all I had left in this world. My complicated feelings of loss and abandonment evolved into sheer anger toward God. I felt like asking this so-called loving God a few questions.

"So *this* is your idea of love? Why are these terrible people still alive while Calvin, the kindest, strongest, most amazing man in the world, is dead?"

I was dealing with issues an adult would struggle to unravel or understand. I also had to survive a rough neighborhood without the man who was teaching me to become one. On top of that, I was still White on the outside and Black on the inside, trying to find my place in the world.

Momma came outside.

"Come on, Son, it's going to be okay."

She was grieving herself, but Momma was there for me, helping me through my most dire time, so now, in her helpless years, I had to make things right with her.

After landing in DC, I picked up my Mercedes and headed to see Momma. She usually felt a little spry after a nap, so I let the caregivers know I'd wait in the parking lot until one of them looked out Momma's window and gave me the thumbs up. I entered with confidence, with a box full of history and proof that I was her son.

I immediately held up a picture of Calvin in his military uniform.

"Man, woman, you had a fine husband!"

Just as I had hoped, she was a bit startled and didn't get the chance to retaliate with one of her racist rants.

"What the...?" Momma said. "I don't know why you so surprised. I was pretty darn fine myself, Mister."

Momma studied the pictures of her and Calvin at a Mason Ceremony.

"That is one good looking Black man right there. And, yeah, that's me, looking good as usual. Don't think because I'm a country girl from Mississippi that I didn't have style."

"Did you say Mississippi? Did you say Mississippi, Momma? I mean Mrs. Studevent!"

Unable to contain my excitement, I excused myself to use the restroom down the hall.

"Hey, call Dr. Oz! Call Dr. Phil! Heck, you can even call Oprah! Alzheimer's can kiss my white-and-black behind!"

My comments confused the staff, but I didn't care. I called Cookie and Linda, who were cautiously optimistic but excited. Feeling an amazing sense of accomplishment, I jokingly told them to refer to me as Dr. Studevent. At last, Lemell Studevent had remembered that she was from Mississippi. Maybe I didn't need to display every piece of memorabilia I had brought.

I walked back into Momma's room.

"Mrs. Studevent, I know you are trying to make sense of all of this, but I want you to look at this picture and tell me what you think."

I showed her a picture of me with the family.

"Is that a White man with all them Black folks?"

Instead of focusing on the picture, she glanced out the window and saw my rental car.

"Is that your Mercedes?"

I nodded.

She looked again and spotted the Mississippi sign. Her demeanor instantly changed and she looked at me stone-cold and gritted her teeth.

"Get out of here right now! Y'all White people get pleasure from playing tricks on me. Y'all think I'm a dumb country backwoods nigga. Don't ever come back!"

She picked up her Bible.

"Mister, now I'm going to spend some time reading about the Lord. I am going to close my eyes and pray that when I open them back up, you'll be long gone."

I quickly came back down to Earth. As I was leaving, I knew I needed to figure out a way to incorporate the Lord into getting her to relax and opening up again about her past. Somehow, I needed to recruit God's help. Did he have a miracle for me? I hoped so.

9

"I lie here sometimes wondering who I am, where I've been, and where I'm going next."

Momma loved the song, "Amazing Grace." She got really emotional hearing it at Calvin and David's funerals. I asked the activities coordinator at her facility if I could bring in the choir from her church to sing to the residents. It would be a nice treat for everyone, and might help me with Momma. I figured, if *AG* doesn't ring some memory bells, then nothing will.

After a little negotiating, the choir agreed. Linda and Cookie were members, which would make it an extra treat for Momma. The full choir was too big and loud, but even half the members could blow the roof off. When Mrs. Dorothy Brooks performed one of her powerful solos, folks would think Aretha Franklin had stopped by.

I asked Dorothy to look at Momma and say these exact words:

"Sister Studevent, your son Raymond requested that I sing that song especially for you."

I felt sure that her acknowledgment that I was Momma's son would at least make her consider the possibility. I promised to treat the choir to dinner and to purchase new robes with their names monogrammed on them if they got Momma to remember anything.

Things got off to a rocky start. Momma was holed up in her room, not feeling well. I couldn't send the choir back, so I arranged for them to sing while Momma stayed in bed with her door open. The choir swayed gracefully back and forth, clapping their hands and launched into a harmonious humming. Just as I suspected, their first run nearly blew the doors off the place. The mailman stopped in his tracks, poked his head in, and tapped his feet along with the choir. Soon, the residents and staff started clapping along.

When it came time for Dorothy's much-anticipated solo, she softly whispered the first lyrics before the choir began humming a sound so beautiful, like a chorus of angels had flown in from heaven for this special occasion. I was mesmerized. As Dorothy headed toward the back of the room, I noticed tears flowing down her face, and as I followed her, I saw why.

Momma was standing in the doorway, trying to clap her hands together and sing. Dorothy put her arm around her and a nurse helped Momma join the front row of the choir. There was not a dry eye in the room. Some of the members were so overcome with emotion their harmonies went out of tune. As soon as they finished, the entire makeshift auditorium erupted in applause.

Mrs. Brooks put her arm around me and looked at Momma.

"Sister Studevent, that song was for you. Your loving son requested it because he knows it's your favorite."

Momma let out a soft chuckle.

"Son, huh? Y'all folks are crazy. Thank you for singing that song. It sounded so beautiful. I've heard it before, but I can't remember when or where."

Everyone sat in silence as the hope and optimism I had felt drained right out of me. As Momma was escorted back to her room, I thanked the choir for their time to perform for Momma and the others. I still treated them to dinner and new robes.

What made this entire situation so frustrating is how it reminded me of the story of my entire life. As a child, my parents didn't want me. Then my uncle died. Then Calvin. Now, the only parent I had didn't know who I was. She could remember Linda and Cookie because she saw them all the time and they had convinced her that they were important people in her life.

Later that evening, I was on the couch at Linda's house, throwing myself a pity party, when a staff member from the facility called, wanting to know if I could come immediately.

When I arrived, the head nurse gestured toward Momma, who was wandering aimlessly down the hall. She had been yelling all evening for the crazy White man who always came to visit. She was bewildered and kept yelling

"Hey, White lady! Where is that crazy White man? He got them devilish blue eyes, but I like him! I need to talk to him because... *Amazing Grace*... yeah, Jesus is amazing."

Her words became slurred as she became more disoriented.

Then Momma saw me.

"Hey you! Come talk to me! Why did you leave me earlier? Aren't you supposed to be my son? I know it's crazy, but I think God is using you to help me overcome my bad feelings about White folks. I can't get into the pearly gates of heaven without making things right with the Lord. Jesus is helping me understand that all White folks ain't bad. Some o' y'all even want to be Black, ain't that right?"

I helped her walk to her room. As we made our way with the walker, she stopped and stared at her hand as if it had just sprouted an extra finger. My large White hand was on top of hers, trying to keep her standing up straight.

"Lord have mercy," she said.

Back in her room, I asked her why she thought God was helping her overcome her racist attitude concerning White people.

"No matter how hard I try, I can't seem to remember anything. But the one thing I do remember is that I've always had a real problem with White folks, especially blue-eyed ones."

I sat there stunned because I had never been able to make sense of how Momma couldn't remember anyone, but she could recall the fact that White people had mistreated her. It made me think of the old Maya Angelou quote, "I've learned that people will forget what you said, people will forget what you did, but people will never forget how you made them feel."

I walked to the window and saw a beautiful, star-studded evening sky, which lifted my spirits even more. I stared at it for several minutes before bringing it to Momma's attention.

"Somebody told me it says in the Bible that God knows each and every star by name," she said. "He also created the rainbow as a reminder about the promise made to never destroy the Earth again with a flood. Yeah, one of them Jehovah's Witnesses came by and told me that during a group Bible study."

Ironically, she didn't remember that I was actually one of Jehovah's Witnesses, so I knew she really *had* lost much of her memory. I laughed a little.

"Oh, so now you're studying with Jehovah's Witnesses? Girl, you really are trying to get it right with God. You reading the Quran, too?"

Hoping to take advantage of her newfound warmth, I sat next to her and held her hand.

"The Lord gonna close the gates on you," I said, "so you better treat this White man good. Now that the fear of Jesus is getting you to act right by me, let's *really* talk."

I had used the reverence she had for God against her, which didn't go over well. Even if it was wrong, I had to take advantage of this opportunity to have a courageous conversation.

"Momma, do you really think I would pretend to be your son if it weren't true? I've never tried to convince you that you're my mother. All these visits have been more to convince you that you're the most incredible woman I've ever known. God may not like your attitude toward White people, but there's no disputing the fact that you have so much goodwill in your heavenly bank account with Him that I'm sure you are fine in His eyes and as long as you continue to study the Bible with Jehovah's Witnesses, you will be fine by Him."

She didn't respond so I continued.

"You might not like White folks, but you could have easily given me back to my heroin addicted White mother, especially after that handsome husband of yours passed away. Instead of taking the easy way out, you decided the Christian thing to do was adopt his nephew and raise him as your own. What you did speaks volumes about the kind of person you are."

To my surprise, my sister had found an old copy of my birth certificate. Anxious to present my greatest piece of evidence to date, I pulled out a piece of neatly folded paper, carefully unfolded it and positioned it at eye level for us both to see.

"This here is my birth certificate. Look at the names. Father: Calvin Studevent, Mother: Lemell Studevent. Child: Raymond Lorenzo

Studevent. Do you notice how in the race box I was identified as Negro?"

She looked at it long and hard as her hand trembled uncontrollably.

"Let me ask you a question," she said. "See that picture up on the wall? What color are Jesus' eyes?"

Before I could respond, Momma answered her own question.

"Blue. I suppose if Jesus really has blue eyes then it would be a sin to hate my savior when I see him."

We started to laugh about what she had said.

"Boy, I still have absolutely no idea who the hell you are, but I like you."

She grabbed my hand.

"I want to thank you for all you've done for me these past few months. You bring me pictures of a handsome man, choirs, birth certificates, and all I can say is, if it ain't true, then you sure is one crazy White man. But you have made me feel like a woman who had it going on at one time in her life. And for that, young man, I want to thank you. I lay here sometimes wondering who I am, where I've been, and where I'm going next. But now that I know I got a fine handsome Black man waiting for me in heaven, well, I better start loving White people so I can get up there to him. By the way, I kinda suspected you might be one of us the first time you came calling. After you left, I stood in the window and saw you drive off in that Cadillac. I said to myself, that boy drives that Caddy like a brotha'. Just a leanin' all down the side of that seat, with his head bobbing back and forth."

She had obviously forgotten that we had already had the Cadillac discussion.

We talked for a good while until Momma fell asleep. I pulled the blanket up and massaged her hands until the caregiver told me that visiting hours were over. I kissed Momma on the forehead and just as I was about to exit, she unexpectedly whispered to me.

"Hey, you come back and see me real soon, you hear me, boy."

I ran back and hugged her tight. The caretaker started to close the curtains, but I asked her to leave them open so the moonlight could shine in on Momma. As I walked down the hallway with tears streaming down my face, the facility's security guard approached.

"Hey, you can stay and watch Mrs. Studevent for a bit. She is something else, ain't she? By the way how do you know her?"

Of course, this crazy day would have to end with somebody questioning me and Momma's relationship.

I was in the mood to chuckle some more, so I answered him.

"Oh, it's dark out here so you can't tell the resemblance, Mrs. Studevent is my Momma."

His eyes grew wide.

"That Black woman in there carried you for nine months?"

I smiled.

"Sir, that incredible woman in there carried me much longer than that. Have a nice evening."

10

"You fight racism by getting good grades and proving White people wrong when they say we are just a bunch of dummies."

I needed a drink. Cookie and Linda would bombard me with questions, so first I had to process the day's events and celebrate a major breakthrough with Momma. As soon as I settled into an isolated spot inside a nearby bar, I pulled out my birth certificate and took a long slug of beer. What would have happened if I had not gone to live with the Studevents? Calvin had saved me, and life changed after he died. It didn't take long before I learned that becoming a man in my neighborhood involved quite a bit of courage.

One night, Momma woke me up.

"Raymond, somebody is in the house downstairs. I just heard them come through the window. I need you to crawl out of your window onto the porch roof and stay there. I am going to call 911."

As she reached for the phone, we heard the burglar slowly creaking up the stairs. As I ducked out the window, I saw him enter Momma's room. She dropped the phone and I started screaming.

"Somebody help us! Call the police! It's a nigga in our house!"

Momma turned on the lamp and the guy ran downstairs and out of the house. Cookie and Linda came running out of their rooms. I asked Momma if she was mad at me for calling the man a nigga.

"In this case, you can call him anything you want."

That was one of the scariest nights of my life. Soon after, Momma went back to her country roots and bought a snub-nosed .357 magnum. To make sure folks knew she meant business, she made her presence known among the bad guys in the neighborhood. She dragged me along with her down Minnesota Avenue and confronted the thugs standing by Malcolm's Liquor Store.

"I don't know and I don't care if any of you had anything to do with the recent neighborhood break-ins. If you have, or you know who did, I want you fellows to give them a warning from me."

Then she handed one of them a bullet.

"You will come in vertical but go out horizontal, with a sheet over you. My husband just died, and he worked too hard to provide us with that home. Any one of y'all niggas break in my house, you will join him in the ground. The only difference will be, he'll be looking down on me from up there, but you will be looking up from hell."

The guys just stared at Momma. Me, too.

"And I had better not hear of any of you giving this boy a hard time. That would qualify you for a similar fate. Come on Raymond."

Momma made it clear that anyone in her path would catch her wrath in the form of a bullet. Our house was never broken into again, but the next few months were filled with problems. On what would have been Calvin's forty-eighth birthday, Momma was planning to visit his grave site for the first time. The cemetery had notified her that the headstone had been placed.

Early that morning, she got a phone call and learned that her father had passed away that morning. She agonized on whether or not to go to his funeral. I thought the only reason Momma didn't want to go was because she couldn't stand the thought of visiting the place where her husband and brother had recently died. She later told me she was afraid to leave us in the house alone because she heard there were still cat burglars lurking in the neighborhood, brazenly breaking into homes in the middle of the night. She ultimately went, but later admitted she felt guilty about it.

It was such a difficult period for Momma. Cookie had fallen into a deep depression over Calvin's death. As the spring of 1975 rolled around, things were looking better. Linda was about to graduate from Bowie State University. Everyone was excited because Jesse Jackson was giving the commencement speech. The biggest question around the house was whether Linda's afro was bigger than Jesse's.

Momma finally had something to celebrate. I recall her telling Calvin at his gravesite, "Sweetheart, I made good on the first of two promises. Linda qualified with honors to graduate in a month. Our oldest will walk across the stage and get her degree. After she graduates, I promise I will begin the process to adopt Raymond."

The following week tragedy struck again. A drunk driver smashed into Linda's car at high speed and her back and both legs were broken. When Momma, Cookie and I arrived at the hospital, the doctors weren't sure if she would ever walk again. Momma was facing the prospect of having a paraplegic daughter.

I hated visiting Linda because it reminded me of all the times I spent there as a young child, when I saw Linda with tubes in her face and straps on her legs.

Linda could barely talk but she gave me instructions.

"Scoop, get my pick."

I asked her which comb and she held up a fist, letting me know to bring her afro pick with the Black fist and the penny melted into it. She was definitely "Soul Sister Number One."

"Scoop, you are a Studevent now, right? You are a part of this family. Alright then, I need you to prove your allegiance by making sure that my afro is bigger than Jesse's. Every time you come visit, I want you to pick it out."

"But the doctors said you won't be able to walk for six months.

"Let Momma handle that."

The doctors and Momma didn't agree on the prognosis. She kept telling them about Linda's upcoming graduation. She always dragged me along during those encounters. People got confused when she told them I was her son. I was nervous because the doctors were White and I suspected Momma would make it a racial issue.

"Ms. Studevent," a doctor said, "I know you and your daughter really want her to attend her graduation, but she barely escaped paralysis."

"Doctor, first I want to say thank you for keeping my baby from spending her life in a wheelchair. I believe the Lord used you to keep her walking. Now as far as this graduation. First, I am a Southern woman from Mississippi, not too fond of White folks, because well, Mississippi in the thirties and forties. Enough said. My folks had dreams of us making it to college. I made it to the tenth grade because we needed me to work so we could survive."

The doctor was listening, maybe for his own protection.

"I promised my late husband that I would make sure to see Linda graduate and that I would place a picture of her walking across that stage on his grave. I am also going to make a Xerox copy of her diploma and place it there as well. That's why I need you to see to it that she can get away to go across that stage."

After thinking it through for a few minutes, the doctor said, "Would it count if she went across in a wheelchair?"

"I don't care if she has to crawl like a seal across there, as long as she gets that piece of paper. I am willing to sign any documents clearing you of any liability if she falls or something."

The doctor agreed that Linda could go home in a wheelchair a week before the graduation so she could get comfortable.

On June 7, 1975, Jesse Jackson gave the commencement speech at Bowie State University. Linda not only crossed the stage in her wheelchair; she took a picture with Jesse Jackson, and more important, her afro dwarfed his.

"Right on sista'," said Jesse, which became the highlight of the ceremony.

True to her word, on July 4, 1975, one year after Calvin's death, Momma placed a copy of Linda's college diploma on his grave.

Over time, Momma stopped linking me with what White folks had done to her family. She realized she could not sit in the Lord's house every Sunday and claim to be a Christian if she did not make good on the promise she made to Calvin. I wanted to be adopted. Despite being so young, I knew it was the right thing for Momma to do. Some things in life are easy to figure out.

First, she had to get my birth mother and father to sign the adoption papers. Momma called them "junkie and drunkie" because, according to her, they didn't deserve to be referred to as "Momma and Daddy." After a citywide search, she found Jackie in an abandoned alley. She declined to sign the papers because she was receiving welfare benefits from the city based on being my parent. It took some doing, but Momma finally convinced her.

I was in the car with Linda and Cookie. Always loving a good argument, they rolled the windows down so we could all hear. I felt torn and sad because I could barely recognize the beautiful woman I had known when I was younger.

Jackie was irritated and started off on the wrong foot.

"Well, if it ain't the country, uppity fancy dressed Mississippi Negro here to tell me I am an unfit mother. How can you be uppity and country?"

"Listen to me Jackie, here is the lawyer's office address and phone number, I hope you don't make this harder than it needs to be. I didn't come here to argue. I just want you to sign the papers so I can carry out Calvin's wishes."

"Hmm, now you about to see what life is like without a man?"

Momma instantly became "Momma" when she heard that snide remark.

"Listen, junkie!"

"My name is Jackie, not junkie!"

"You ought to be glad I didn't call you a honky, better yet what you are, a honky junkie. Jackie, Cracker, whatever!"

"Oh, just like a good Mississippi Mamie, you want to take care of the little White kid for us White folks?"

Momma's blood pressure hit the "last nerve" and it was on!

"Raymond come here!"

Cookie and Linda were anxious to jump into the fray, but Momma told them to get back in the car.

"Don't yell at my Scoop like that, woman!"

"Your Scoop! Your Scoop!"

Momma grabbed my hand.

"Look at your Scoop's fingernails! Look at that cut on his lip! Rub the back of his head. Feel that, it's fractured skull. Somehow, nobody seems to know how that happened. Oh, wait! Maybe he fell off the bed after he killed his brother Howard! Y'all blamed this boy for doing that and every single time you drive, oh wait, you don't even drive. Well, every time your bus or taxi goes past Howard University, right there, I want you to remember what you did and how you traumatized this boy."

Jackie was visibly upset.

"Woman please, Scoop was too young to remember all that stuff."

The argument Momma had hoped to avoid was happening, but it gave her a chance to finally release her pent-up resentment.

"Too young? You remember the game Hide and Seek? Raymond can't play Hide and Seek. You know why? Because he is too afraid to crawl under a bed, a car or inside a closet."

"I think he is crostraphobic," Jackie said.

"First of all, the word is claustrophobic, and it doesn't apply in Raymond's case. The word you're looking for is traumatized."

Jackie was street wise and sharp-tongued, too, and had a lethal response for Momma.

"Scoop don't need you, because no matter how good a life you give him, you and I both know that I gave him something more valuable than you uppity Negroes could ever do. I gave him those beautiful blue eyes and milky White skin. So, Ms. Mell, we both know that he got it made in this White man's world, whether you raise him, or I do."

"Your White skin and blue eyes? I see that they worked out just fine for you now, haven't they, Jacqueline?"

What happened next explains the unique brilliance of Lemell Studevent. In an effort to calm her nerves, she lit a cigarette and offered Jackie one.

"Here. Come on, Jackie, I know life ain't been easy and I heard at twelve years old you had to leave home to keep that evil stepdaddy of yours from pushing up on you."

Momma's empathy took Jackie by surprise.

"Yeah, I'm sorry about them country comments, I know you good folk, Mell. Can I get a couple of smokes?"

"No problem, you meet me at the lawyer's office on Friday and I will bring you a full carton. What do you smoke?"

Jackie smiled with excitement.

"Kools!"

Lemell laughed because that was a popular brand amongst Black folks.

"Of course you do! Now, if you want that carton, I need a favor. Tell me where that boy's crazy daddy hangs out."

Jackie gladly spilled the beans.

"Tuesdays and Thursday nights, he plays at The Chateau on Benning Road, a few blocks from your house. I asked him why he won't come see Scoop."

"You mean to tell me that Raymond plays twice a week three blocks from my house?" Alright, I gotta go, Friday at the law office, one o'clock sharp, come pick up your carton."

Momma and I went to The Chateau, which turned out to be the most humiliating moment in my young life and still ranks high on my most hurtful list. It also turned out to be a most gratifying and memorable night.

They wouldn't let Momma take me inside because it was an adult establishment. Then an older lady recognized Momma and pointed out that the owner knew her from the library.

"Hey, Mrs. Studevent. I am so sorry to hear about your husband passing last year," he said. "You know I could lose my liquor license if I let you bring that boy inside."

"Look, see that nigga on stage? That's my nephew, and as you can see by his son who I'm trying to adopt, he done messed around uptown. I need him to sign these adoption papers and bring them to my lawyer."

"Hmm, oh, okay, he one of them type Negroes, by all means let that fool have it. I can't wait to see this. Access granted and let the fun begin."

He was playing The Temptations current hit song, "Papa Was a Rolling Stone," which is about a man who had a bunch of children out of wedlock and never took care of any of them. As he finished the song, he spotted us standing nearby. I was pleasantly surprised because one of his singers was Aunt Connie.

Being the egotistical showoff that he was, he jumped into full character.

"Oh wow! Folks we are in for a special treat tonight. I am so happy to introduce y'all to my aunt right there and my son, Raymond Junior! She brought him here to see his daddy perform tonight. Junior, come on up here. As y'all can tell, I been around uptown a bit doing my part in the integration program the president was talking about. Come on, Junior."

Momma and I looked at each other.

"I got this Momma. You taught me well."

He picked me up and sat me on the edge of the stage next to him. He was in Negro heaven. Everyone there that night got to see him show off his White son. Just as I expected and frankly hoped he would do, he offered me the mic.

"You wanna say anything to these good folks who came to see your daddy perform?"

I took the mic and jumped down from the stage.

"My daddy. My daddy? You're my Black daddy with the big brown Caddy. You drive by my street a least once a week and you never stop once to say hello to your White trophy son. I seen you about fifty times and you ain't talked to me more than three times in all my life."

While I was talking, I overheard a bystander approach Momma.

"Hey lady, how come he speaks so mature for his age?"

"The boy been to hell and back because of his deadbeat parents. He had to grow up fast."

I walked over to her.

"Momma, can I have special permission to use that word?"

She nodded. I looked back at him and didn't waste a second.

"Nigga, please!"

I saw the disgust on Momma's face so I asked her if she had anything to say. She took the mic and proceeded to put on a short, but masterful verbal undressing that will live forever in The Chateau's Hall of Fame.

"Let me congratulate my nephew first. He sang the right song, because he is a rolling stone. Boy got kids all over DC and don't take care of any of them. Boy got white, yellow, brown, dark-skinned kids. Don't matter to him. Sounds good, but that ain't even the worst of it. How many of you know our local DC gal, Connie Christmas?"

The people start catcalling as soon as they heard Momma mention her name. She had to pause before continuing.

"Yeah, she's a friend of mine. As a matter of fact, she is singing here tonight. Mr. Spotlight man, put the light on the backup singers."

The bright lights exposed Connie, whose face and lips were obviously swollen.

"Y'all wanna know why she's so far back? Step out here, Girl. Look at her face. That's because ole' Deadbeat Daddy with the Caddy is beating her up."

People started booing and walking out. My father jumped down into Lemell's face.

"You Aunt Jemima country nigga. Whatcha think you doing? Trying to ruin me."

Momma didn't back down.

"Negro, don't think because Calvin is dead you can run up on me. I got four country brothers that will slice you like a pig in a slaughterhouse. Sign these papers and you ain't got to worry about me anymore. Otherwise, I will make your life as a two-bit singer all but over."

She handed him the adoption papers.

"I better see you next Friday. You can see your lovely uptown White girl while you at it."

When Momma and I got in the car, we shared a defining moment in our relationship.

"I am so proud of how you let him have it in there," she said. "He deserved it."

I shrugged my shoulders. She noticed me looking out the window.

"What's wrong Raymond? Look at me, Son."

I was crying.

"It doesn't matter how much we get him or my mother. They don't want me and they don't love me. I didn't deserve to be born with this curse of looking White and being Black. I hate it. Daddy is gone forever, and I just wish my parents would love me, even if they can't raise me. At least come say hi or something. Why! Why Momma?"

At that moment, my father walked out the back door. I jumped out of the car and screamed at him through all my tears.

"I hate you! I hate you!"

Then I spit on his Cadillac.

"Son! Junior!"

"Son? Junior? Fool, I don't even know you and you will forget me the minute you leave here. But not tonight!" I picked up a rock and threw it through his windshield.

"Tell people your White son did it! The one named Raymond. That should be easy to remember with all your kids. Your name is the only thing you ever gave me. When I get grown, I'm changing it."

Momma hugged me.

That night, I realized that no matter how happy I was to be with her, I was traumatized from being abandoned by my biological parents.

Needless to say, we celebrated when they signed the papers. Momma and I were developing a special relationship and she slowly became my new hero. While she held back from embracing me fully, her decency began to shine.

While I had plenty of friends to play with, I remained sad and lonely inside. In order to cope, I created two imaginary friends, one Black and one White. I would hang with one of them one day and the other the next.

"Who are you talking to?" Momma would say.

I start singing my imaginary dialogue so if she or anyone else saw me talking to myself, it would appear as though I was singing.

I was hyper, with a short attention span, so I often got in trouble for doing stupid things. Once, I hit a neighbor in the head with an apple and Momma made me go to the library with her every day throughout the summer. I must have read 200 books!

My grades were always good, though, so Momma could never complain. She asked me how things were at school, knowing that my complexion was problematic. Although I survived most days without incident, she took matters into her own hands on one occasion.

Roots, the TV series based on Alex Haley's acclaimed novel, was stirring up a lot of emotion in our home and in the community. I mentioned that our homework was to watch its debut on Sunday and write down our thoughts. Momma didn't wait. Instead of requesting a meeting with my teacher and the principal she marched directly into my classroom on Friday and whispered a few things to my teacher, Mrs. Bowman, who appeared irritated that Momma was going to address the classroom.

"This weekend, some of you are going to watch *Roots.* Some of you may be upset and rightfully so. You may want to take out some of that anger on someone. There's only one kid in this room who looks White. I said *looks* White. Raymond is my son. Get the confused look off your faces. If you want to fight him one on one, he will be more than happy to beat your butt. But you fight racism by getting good grades and proving White people wrong when they say we are just a bunch of dummies. You don't accomplish anything by attacking a classmate. Thank you, Mrs. Bowman. Have a nice weekend everybody, and enjoy *Roots.*"

11

*"That's my son. I don't care
what papers I signed and what
those White folks downtown
have to say."*

I was eleven years old, and Calvin had been dead for four years.
The adoption seemed to be a forgone conclusion, but my biological father had other ideas. One cold winter evening, while my
friends and I were playing football in the street, a Cadillac Fleetwood
swung around the corner until the driver slammed on the brakes and
rolled down the window. I immediately recognized my father's car. A
plume of cigarette smoke wafted out of it as I heard his voice.

"Get in the car!"

Unsure what to do, I wiped the sweat from my face and stood
motionless.

"Boy, I am yo' daddy, get in this car, now!"

I jumped in the back seat, wondering what he wanted. He hit the
gas and sped away. I could barely see his face in the rearview mirror
through all the smoke.

"Boy, you're my son. I'm the HNIC around here—Head Nigga in Charge! Let's go get some McDonald's."

To this day, it seems like all deadbeat dads use McDonald's to ingratiate themselves to their children. Happy Meals seem to work for little girls, and after the age of seven, fathers always opt to bond over a Big Mac.

I suppose I should have been traumatized by the enormity of the moment, but the first five years of my life had immunized me from responding as a normal kid my age. When we got to his apartment, he called Lemell and started yelling.

"That's my son. I don't care what papers I signed and what those White folks downtown have to say."

I kept thinking about how angry and hurt Momma must be. I wanted to call her, but I was terrified, afraid of her reaction and scared that this crazy man known as my father might lose his temper if he caught me. I thought he might be still mad that I had cracked his windshield and embarrassed him in front of a live audience.

Just like old times, I slept on a couch in a one-bedroom apartment, in Eastgate, one of DC's most notorious housing projects. Everyone called it "The Gate," as in the gates of hell, just what a white Negro child needs after finally finding stability.

I knew that the moment I stepped outside I would have to fight for respect. Oddly, I had no problems. I found out later that Raymond had sent word around the neighborhood that anyone giving me a hard time would have to deal with him. I wasn't called Scoop, Ben, Ray or even White boy. I was effectively known as "Frank's son."

While Raymond was a relative stranger to me, I discovered he was given the name Frank by local gangsters because he reminded them of Al Capone's hit man, Frank Nitti, who also had a hot temper and was a great dresser.

Could this man who I resembled so much actually be a family man now? I thought.

He brought Connie's daughter, Yolanda, over on weekends and he had a one-year-old with a new girlfriend. I was fascinated by Nikia, my new little sister. Playing with her provided a distraction from the reality of my confusing circumstances. Frank's personality was so domineering that I could never formulate an opinion regarding right and wrong.

Any glimmer of optimism that he had changed was quickly erased when I witnessed him smash Nikia's mother in the face. He beat her up the same way he abused Connie. The trauma of being around a violent drunk was much worse than anything I had experienced living with my biological mother. I grew terrified of this man and his fiery temper and began once again to bite my fingernails at a feverish pace.

One day, he took Nikia from her mother and calmly handed her to me.

"Here, Junior, hold your sister."

Then he turned and punched her mother in the face with a closed fist, dragged her down the hallway and began beating her with a crowbar. He broke her nose and ankle that day.

The nerve of him to call me Junior when I had only seen him a handful of times! But I was so afraid of him, he could have called me anything. He seemed to take pride in using words, such as Junior, Sister and Daddy. It was as if he were creating an imaginary family in his mind.

Some consider any man who beats up a woman to be a coward, that it makes them feel like a man. While Raymond was despicable in that regard, and that assumption may often be true, he was certainly no coward.

He had a younger brother, named Ollie, who stood about six foot five. Raymond was five foot ten. One evening, Ollie confronted Raymond about how wrong he was for defying the courts and kidnapping me from Lemell. Ollie stood over Raymond in such a menacing way, I thought he might have the courage to stand up to him.

"Brother, you are as wrong as two left feet and you need to take that boy home to Aunt Lemell's house. You're thirty-eight years old! Who do you think you are? Thirty-eight!"

Raymond stood there and politely and calmly placed his Colt 45 beer on the table. He tilted his head sideways to light a cigarette.

"Thirty-eight?" he said softly. "Hmm, excuse me for a moment."

He returned quickly from the bedroom and told me to turn the volume down on the television so I could hear what the HNIC was about to say. I sat on the couch, holding Nikia in one hand and biting my nails on the other.

In a gangster move that would have made Capone and Frank Nitti proud, Raymond displayed a pistol in each hand and a cigarette hanging from his bottom lip. He stretched up to reach Ollie's temple, slowly pressed the tip of a pearl handled .38 caliber pistol into Ollie's skull, and calmly walked him to the door.

"Now, what were you saying about this thirty-eight? Cain killed Abel, and from one brother to another, if you ever come over here and tell me about my son, they gonna be tagging your toe."

He never removed the cigarette from his mouth and ashes fell on the floor. Toe-tagging referred to how coroners tagged the toe of corpses to identify the body.

While I thought the matter was settled, Raymond demonstrated how ruthless he could be. He put one pistol in his waist, opened the door and plucked his cigarette into the hallway.

"Now, because you made me waste a cigarette and my beer got warm, you go down to the liquor store and get me a six pack of Colt and a full carton of Kool's."

He then turned back to me.

"Junior, what's your favorite candy?"

I sputtered for a second.

"Now and Laters."

"What flavor?"

"Watermelon."

"Watermelon." Raymond laughed.

"See, I told y'all he was a nigga. Get Nikia a lollipop. You got fifteen minutes."

When Ollie returned in what felt like three minutes. Raymond continued showing off his gangster side.

"Put my beers in the fridge and open me up a cold one and don't spill any suds on my floor. Open up my smokes, light me up a square and put the lollipop in my baby's mouth."

While this modern-day Cain didn't kill Abel, he sure did humiliate him. It was like David had reduced Goliath from a tiger to a pussycat.

The final straw for me came soon after, as I stood on the front stairs of the apartment building one day, watching Raymond run after a bus while shooting his gun in the air and yelling at a guy for whistling at Nikia's mother. That's when I began putting my escape plan together. I figured I had to make my move while Raymond was at work. Momma said she couldn't come get me because her lawyer had advised her to wait and let the judicial system run its course. It would not look good for her to go and snatch me like Raymond did.

One night, it started to snow. I prayed that it wouldn't keep Raymond and his girlfriend from going to work the next day. If they did, I could escape. I don't think I prayed that hard since I begged God to keep Calvin alive. The following morning, I saw that the snow had piled up so I figured Raymond wouldn't go to work. I punched the couch and cried from disappointment.

About an hour later, much to my surprise, I heard Raymond getting ready to leave. I pretended to be asleep as he and his girlfriend walked out. I was too young to babysit Nikia, so I stayed alone, ready to make my getaway like Julia Roberts did in *Sleeping with the Enemy*.

All I needed was confirmation from Momma. I knew that a snowstorm would never keep her home from work, so I called to tell her that it would take about an hour for me to walk home in the snow. She offered to pick me up halfway, but I was so frightened to escape that I screamed at her that I had to leave immediately.

"Okay, Baby, you be careful, and I should be home around the same time you arrive."

Hearing the joy in her voice made me hurry. I shoved my toys in one of Raymond's suitcases while I sang the old Negro spiritual, "Go Down Moses (Let My People Go)!" It had only been a few months but living with Raymond felt like I'd survived four hundred years of oppression, like the Israelites and Negroes.

I left Raymond a note and headed toward home.

"Sorry, Raymond, I am going back to my Momma. Please stop drinking alcohol. It makes you a monster."

Within twenty minutes, I realized the first wave of trauma one experiences when escaping an abusive situation. My fingers and toes began to feel numb, so I stopped a few times to warm up in convenience stores. My tears froze on my cheeks as I dragged the suitcase through the snow, thinking how Raymond would react when he realized I had gone back to Lemell's.

After nearly an hour, I crept over the hill and began to feel warm because I could see Momma sitting in her car, trying to stay warm. I wanted to stop crying so she wouldn't think I was a wimp, but I was overwhelmed. Although my coat was zipped up like an Eskimo, I could see her wiping the mist from the inside of her Cadillac's windshield, trying to see if it was me. I barely raised a frozen arm to give her a thumbs up.

I dropped the suitcase as soon as she jumped out of the car and ran to meet me. We embraced and fell in the snow, laughing and crying.

"Lord, I missed you, Boy."

"Momma, I am so sorry! I'm so sorry, I was just scared. I didn't mean to hurt you!"

She wiped away her tears with her gloves.

"I know, Baby, I know. Let's get you in the house and Momma is going to make you your favorite dinner. What do you want?"

I wiped my nose on my sleeve.

"Two words Momma. Sweet'ata pie."

"How about some good ol' Mississippi down home Southern fried chicken? And then a sweet'ata pie, all for you! I knew the Lord would answer my prayers and bring you home."

Momma shoved me in her warm car.

I couldn't help asking a buzzkill question.

"What if Raymond comes over and starts breaking bad?"

Momma laughed.

"He ain't badder than the Lord, and besides, he ain't driving over here in the snow."

Up to that point, life had taught me to expect the unexpected, but I hoped she was right.

I took a nice hot shower. After dinner, as I was eating some sweet potato pie, we heard a hard knock on the door. I looked out the window and started shaking because it appeared that Raymond had been drinking and was not happy. When he saw me, I nearly peed in my pants.

"Open this door now, Boy!"

I thought Momma was going to call the police. I ran into the kitchen.

"Momma it's Raymond and he looks crazy."

I noticed a Bible on the counter, and she was staring into the sink as if she was praying.

"Let him in. Heavenly Father…"

I slowly opened the door, and he pushed his way past me and threw his hat on the table.

"Woman, do you know who I am and how many people fear me in these streets?"

Momma sat calmly in her favorite chair next to the utility chest.

"If you was so bad why didn't you try to take that boy when Calvin was alive? You're a typical coward, beating up on helpless women. You knew Calvin would have killed you, but Calvin lives in me and I made him a promise that I would finish what we started and that is to make sure that your son has a decent chance in this world."

Raymond unbuttoned his long coat as if to possibly reach for something.

"Calvin should have beat you, because ain't no woman ever talked to me like that without gettin' a backhand."

"That's because you ain't met the right one yet, but you lookin' at one right now. That's right. Raymond Lorenzo Studevent Senior, you so much as move your hand anywhere near your waist, I will bring an end to your miserable, pathetic life."

Momma opened a drawer and pulled out her .357 magnum and slowly placed it on the kitchen counter beside her Bible. She normally kept her gun next to her bed, but she was ready for Raymond because she had gotten a tip from Nikia's mother that he was on his way.

He held up both palms and assured Momma that he was reaching for his smokes. In a bizarre moment of unexpected kindness, she threw him her lighter so he could light his cigarette.

"Okay, Fool, I am going to put this gun back in the drawer because it has no business being next to the Bible. Are we good, Raymond?"

He took a long drag on his cigarette.

"Negro, I said, are we good?"

He looked at me as if he realized that I knew the truth about him. He dropped his head and nodded to Momma.

"Yeah, we good Lemell."

"Look at me, Raymond."

He cleared his throat as the tears began. Lemell Studevent proceeded to show me what made her the most amazing woman I have ever known. Recognizing that Raymond was about to break down, she preserved his dignity when she could have absolutely humiliated him.

"Raymond, you and this child's mother were both only twelve years old when you were forced to leave home. So I know you didn't have a fair shake in this world. You and her had no business having this child. First of all, interracially messing around in 1966. While I understand that the drinking and drugs are a result of you and Jackie's childhood demons, neither of you has been able to overcome them. Now, if you get yourself together, I promise to allow you to spend some time with your son. I am not going to deprive him of quality time with his father, who happens to be his Black twin. But you have to put that liquor away first."

Raymond said nothing.

"Come here, Boy."

He sighed and walked over to Momma. She gave him a hug and then looked at me.

"Come here little boy."

I joined in on the hug, but what I remember most is feeling his pistol sticking up from the back of his pants. I discovered later that he didn't go to work that day. Instead, he parked his car right around the corner and resumed an affair he was having with a woman in our building. I realized my escape was scarier than I thought because I walked right past her apartment door as I dragged my suitcase down the stairs.

Unfortunately, my relationship with Momma was not quite the same for a while because she felt somewhat betrayed, that I should have refused to go with my father in the first place. I still regret that decision. I should have stood up to Raymond, and more important, I should have stood up for the woman who took on the challenge and responsibility of raising me.

In the end, my father gave up fighting for me, moved to Chicago, and I didn't see him again for sixteen years. After his departure, Momma and I began to bond because Linda and Cookie moved to California. Cookie attended San Jose State University and Linda moved out there after she earned a master's degree from Howard University. Up until then, we had only interacted with Black folks for the most part. But soon, White folks entered the picture, and I came to realize that while Momma was out of Mississippi, Mississippi was definitely not out of Momma.

12

"I like my coffee like this woman lying right here—Black and strong."

A s I finished my beer and a trek down memory lane, my
phone rang.

"Mr. Studevent, Lemell won't go to sleep and she refuses
to take her medication unless you come tell her some more stories.
She wouldn't watch the movie we played for her. She kept complaining that all we have are movies for old White folks."

"You have old classics, right? Do you have *Butch Cassidy and the
Sundance Kid*?"

"Sweetheart, are you kidding me? With Robert Redford and Paul
Newman? Our female residents love that movie. Some of them can't
remember their own names but they identify with those two. I'll have
it for you at the back door. Don't come to the front because I don't
want the others to see Lemell getting a visitor during non-visiting
hours."

I could hardly wait to see Momma's response to Paul Newman,
if she had one. I had no idea what I was hoping to accomplish, and
while I felt a tad bit optimistic after she recalled Mississippi and a few

other things, I was definitely feeling the effects of all these trips into the archives of my brain.

Momma was deteriorating. The voice of pessimism had slowly crept in, no matter how much I tried to avoid hearing it.

When I opened Momma's door, she greeted me joyfully.

"Hey, Calvin. Come sit right here and tell me some more funny stories about the amazing Black woman adopting some unwanted White kid who is really Black or whatever science-fiction tales you got for your Momma today. Got any more stories about how incredible I was for adopting you? Come on now, I'm getting old and I want to remind the Lord of the good things I did so I can get through those pearly gates."

I laughed, choosing to ignore the fact that she'd just called me Calvin.

I inserted the DVD, which the nurse had given me, and fast-forwarded to the first closeup of Paul Newman I could find and hit pause. His eyes were piercing through the screen and I looked to see Momma's reaction.

"Calvin, honey, I don't want to watch any boring movies, I thought you came here to tell me some crazy stories about me being your mother."

I made some small talk, but I wanted to see how she would respond to Paul Newman's piercing blue eyes glaring at her. I kept glancing at the television, hoping she would see him.

"Are you sure you don't want to watch a little bit of this movie? It's really good."

"I don't like cowboy movies, Son."

I was so tired that I didn't even address the fact that she referred to me as Son. I thought it might confuse her even more.

As she began staring at Paul Newman, I couldn't resist the temptation to tease Momma about her past crush on him.

"I know Momma. I know, but it's okay."

"Why are you whispering and what are you talking about?"

"I know you like Paul Newman. Nothing wrong with that."

"Paul who? The only Paul I know is the apostle Paul right here in the good book."

"That White man right there, Paul Newman, the actor. I see you staring at him."

Obviously amused that she'd been caught, Momma laughed.

"Boy, get outta here. Okay, you saw me looking at the White man named Butch, and yeah, he sure is good looking. But you better not tell. Black folks be mad at me."

"How do you know his name is Butch?"

"Listen here, I wanted you to come here and tell me some stories, not play some dumb name game. Heck, I barely know my own."

She looked at the screen and remained quiet. In a rare and awkward moment of direct contact, she looked right into my eyes. I was afraid she was on the verge of another Mississippi flashback and would start screaming hysterically as she had before. I felt a sudden wave of sadness as I saw the frustration in her glaucoma covered eyes.

Visibly shaken by the moment, she stared at me.

"Who am I? Calvin, who are you? Is this some cruel trick? Is this some sort of dream? Are you telling me that I don't remember who I am, what happened over the past how many years? How old am I, anyway?"

"You're eighty-eight years old."

"When I was a child, I always asked God to let me live to be a hundred. You think I will make it, young man?"

"Oh yeah easily. The doctors say you got plenty of years left."

I'm getting sleepy, Calvin. I'm tired and if the Lord wants me home then I think I'm ready to meet Jesus."

My sadness was growing, and it was all I could do to hide it from her.

"What can I do at this moment to help you?"

"The first thing you need to do is turn off that television because between those blue eyes and yours staring at me, I'm getting nervous. The second thing you can do is put me to sleep with your crazy stories. Did you go into the military or college or what?"

I asked the nurse to bring me a blanket and a cup of strong coffee. Momma couldn't resist chiming in.

"No cream and no sugar," she said. "I like my coffee like this woman lying right here—Black and strong."

I assumed that Momma would fall asleep quickly, but after months of telling her the story of our lives, I had come to realize that the process was quite fascinating and, frankly, therapeutic.

The nurse brought a pillow and blanket and handed me a cup of midnight-colored coffee.

"This coffee is strong enough to keep you up for three days."

Momma leaned her head back, clutched her Bible to her chest and adjusted her do-rag.

"Okay, Blue Eyes. I'm all ears."

I began by answering her earlier question about me going to college or the military.

"Momma, I sort of went to both at the same time."

As she closed her eyes, I continued, half for her and half for me.

Life began to change the day I asked Momma to buy me a pair of Stan Smith Adidas. They cost thirty dollars. She said I had to use my paper route money to buy my own clothes. She wanted me to learn the concept of money and how working hard correlated with being able to buy what I wanted. At that time, the designer jean craze had hit America. When I was twelve, Momma noticed that my grades began to slip, and I was spending lots of time on the phone. Her greatest fear had come knocking, literally and figuratively. Girls!

This prompted a serious conversation.

"Raymond, I've overheard some of your conversations with these little nappy headed girls. They so loose in their hot pants, when they have a baby, even the baby comes out pregnant. If you are not careful, chasing them will get you in a lot of trouble and will eventually be your downfall. Girls and women have kept a lot of men from reaching their full potential."

Momma always tried to shoehorn in a Bible lesson.

"Joseph was a good man. That king's wife was begging for it and yelled rape. They threw him in prison when he ran away because he didn't want to commit a sin against God."

The issue of race often found its way into the equation.

"That's what them White women used to do as well. Always yelling rape on a Black man down South so he could be thrown in jail, just like Joseph."

Momma said that Calvin would be proud of me if I went into the military, especially the Marine Corps. She asked me how I felt about attending a military high school. I had always admired Calvin's uniform, so I wasn't totally opposed until she said it was all boys. I couldn't imagine being in a classroom all day without any girls. On top of that, the school was predominantly White, as in 80 percent. I knew that the way I talked and looked would be a serious problem. I had already experienced that when I visited relatives who had White friends.

Two incidents resolved the issue for me. First, I was jumped by a group of six guys at my junior high school. One of them hit me in the face with brass knuckles and broke my nose. The neighborhood violence was getting out of control and Momma wanted to protect me from becoming a victim like so many other kids.

The second incident happened at Momma's job. One day, she asked a neighbor's son to speak to me about his experience at St. John's College High School, the oldest Army JROTC school in the country. He stopped by the library, wearing his military outfit. All the girls were impressed. I was, too, not with just him, but how the girls reacted. He loved the school, and while there were a few White people who didn't like Black folks, he never had any issues. He warned me that you had to be careful catching the bus through the ghetto because any private school uniform would make you a target for the thugs. That was life in DC for everybody, so I wasn't too concerned about that.

Then he emphasized the most important perk.

"Scoop, the ladies love a man in a uniform."

I was fourteen years old and ready to go to war.

"Private Studevent reporting for duty, Sir!"

I still had not gotten over the death of Calvin, and I wanted to carry on his legacy by pursuing a career as a military man. That sure warmed Momma's heart, to know that I wanted to follow in the footsteps of her late husband.

From the first day, I felt immense pressure to prove that a kid from the impoverished side of town could compete academically with the rich White ones. I also became fascinated that people who looked like me might wind up embracing me as one of their own. I started to wonder what these so-called evil White people were all about, so I befriended a number of White cadets.

Momma was quick to offer me a bit of advice.

"Son, get in where you fit in, but never, and I mean *never*, go along just to get along. Remember Calvin's words. 'Before you can be *the* man you have to first learn to be *a* man.' You are in this military school to become a man, so the best way to start is to stand up like one."

People at the school thought it was peculiar that I talked so much like the Black cadets. Once I realized this, I felt embarrassed by my vernacular and limited vocabulary, so I tried to talk more like the White kids. In order to sound more convincing, I began to read history books and became curious about my White heritage. Momma immediately recognized that I seemed to be on a mission to embrace my "whiteness," so she set out to nip that in the bud.

One day, she came across a summer job application I had filled out and noticed that I had checked "White" in the box that asked for the applicant's race.

"Negro, don't think that because you got straight hair and those blue eyes that you're better than us."

"You told me that those folks aren't hiring Blacks, so I put White on the application."

"Your birth certificate says you a Negro, and don't you ever forget that. I bet you ain't told them White folks at school that you got Black blood running through your veins."

I eventually made friends with several White cadets. I became popular because I knew how to shine brass pendants and shoes better than anyone. I had learned these tricks from Uncle Kenny, a member of the Army's Old Guard. My pants were always creased perfectly and impressed the cadets.

"Studevent's pants can stand up by themselves."

All was going well until I had a rude awakening, when these seemingly nice White cadets who professed to be my friends revealed darker sides of themselves. The first time came when I overheard some of them talking in the locker room.

"Yeah, looks like affirmative action has taken hold up here now," said one. "We didn't have this many niggers last year."

"We can't beat DeMatha in basketball or football," said his friend, "so they went out and brought more of them here. My dad said the school gets government money for each minority they admit. That explains it, because a couple of them can't spell a stop sign so I wonder how they passed the admissions exam."

I often heard White cadets spew horrible racist jokes and make derogatory comments. One day, during uniform inspection, a White cadet started to berate the Black cadets. He ridiculed the size of one Black cadet's lips and teased another about his wide nose.

When I became friends with Black cadets, White cadets began to hassle me.

"Hey Studevent, you're not a nigger, and if you want to earn some stripes around here you need to chill with us. You dig, Bro?"

Black cadets were friendly with the White cadets, but they had no clue how many White cadets were two-faced. I didn't say anything to avoid making problems for myself. I also didn't tell Momma, because it would confirm her suspicions that all White people are prejudiced. I wanted to be accepted and fit in, but instead I simply went along to get along. Soon enough, though, the racial identity crisis I felt began to consume me.

I befriended a White cadet who came from a wealthy family. When I saw Matthew snuggling up to a Black girl after a football game, I was convinced that he wasn't prejudiced. One day, he invited Momma and me to have dinner with his family. I was excited, eager to demonstrate to Momma that some White people welcomed Blacks. When we arrived, a Black butler greeted us and two large Black women served us drinks.

"Oh, you must be Raymond, Matthew's new friend from the South."

Then she looked at Momma.

"Excuse me, Ma'am, the coat room for the servers is down the hall."

Matthew's mother also assumed that Momma was a hired servant. Introducing her as my mother was awkward, but the dinner party proceeded without further incident. While Momma appreciated that the Banks family didn't seem racist, she couldn't handle seeing three Black housekeepers serving these rich White people.

"These folks ain't nothing but fancy slaves."

I was totally relieved because Matthew's family were warm and loving. Later that evening, Momma became upset when she overheard me ask Matthew not to tell the other cadets that I was Black. Matthew agreed, as long as I wouldn't tell anyone that he had a Black girlfriend. Teen years can be brutal, and Matthew and I were both living with secrets.

Every time I began to feel comfortable with the race issue, something happened. One day, a priest teaching at the school noticed me hanging out with my Black friends from our side of town and he called me over.

"Studevent, I think you should act like what you are and not try to be what you're not."

I wanted to believe that a man of God could not have meant what he said, so I let it go and didn't raise a stink.

Coincidentally, Momma met me after school that day. On the way home, I casually mentioned what the priest had said. Before I could finish, she slammed on the brakes.

"Oh, what's his name and what's his room number? I am going back right now!"

"Momma it's too late and the teachers are all gone."

She started humming and squeezing the steering wheel. Then I made a mistake.

"Momma he works in the front office and I don't think he meant it that way."

I was hoping Momma would let it go. I always got nervous when she started humming them old Southern Negro spirituals. I couldn't tell the gospel from the slave songs from the Black power songs. In one breath she'd claim a friend in Jesus, but in the next she'd start singing James Brown's, "Say It Loud—I'm Black and I'm Proud." That usually meant it was time to unload on White folks. Still, I was hoping she would let the matter go.

The following day, I was in military training class when I heard someone yelling.

"Whitey! Hillbilly!"

I realized it was Momma unloading to the office about the priest.

Seconds later, she opened the classroom door. To her surprise, my instructor was a Black man, Sergeant Parker. Momma had an explanation for that, but she wanted to show respect and solidarity with the Black officer in front of White cadets.

Later, she told me what was running through her mind at that precise moment.

"Figures they got the White preacher talking about love and the Black man teaching you kids how to kill."

Momma proceeded to unleash a potent dose of her Southern Black fury.

"Excuse me," she said, acknowledging Parker's stripes. "Sergeant Major, pardon me."

She looked around and pointed her finger at me.

"Raymond, get your butt in that hallway right now!"

"Studevent," a classmate said, "is that your maid talking to you like that?"

Momma felt a need to give me the rundown, so we stepped outside.

"I had to set that fool straight. You listen to me. I want you to show these folks what we're all about. You make Calvin proud; you hear me?"

I nodded.

She wasn't done. As I walked back in the room, Momma, in a moment reminiscent of the barber shop incident from nearly a decade ago, began to ridicule any student she saw laughing.

"Hmm, I ain't never seen so many blue eyes. As I walked in here, something seemed funny. Well, I like to laugh, too, so what was it?"

She looked at the White student who had asked me if Momma was my maid.

"No, I ain't his maid. I'm his Momma, not his Mamie."

White kids questioned adults more than Black kids and he had the nerve to respond.

"But you're Black. How is it possible that you are his mother?"

Momma hit him with a classic line I am sure he still remembers. While obviously taken aback, she respected his courage and knew he was right. She looked at his name tag.

"Young man, Corporal Rhodes, do you like *Star Wars*?"

"Of course, I just saw the new one, *The Empire Strikes Back*."

"Think about this, young man, if Dark Vader, a Black man, can be the White boy, Luke Skywalker's daddy, then how come this Black woman can't be that White kid's mother?"

Unfortunately, another cadet felt the need to join in. He was the only Asian kid in the class and apparently had no idea how to deal with a Black woman, so he learned the hard way.

"It's Darth Vader," he said. "Darth, with a 'th,' not 'Dark.'"

"Listen here, Bruce Lee," said Momma.

"Bruce Lee was Chinese. I am Korean."

"Oh really! Well, Officer Lonely, with the one li'l private stripe on your arm. Private Korea! My husband lost two friends in the Korean War and was nearly killed himself so that your folks could come here and not be taken over by Communists. As for Dark Vader, I know it's Darth, but I call him Dark because he acts like a Black man in the movie. He wasn't in his child's life for twenty years and then the fool comes back, saying, 'Luke, I'm yo' Daddy!' So even in outer space, Hollywood got the Black man being a deadbeat dad!"

Then, Momma eyed a Black student, named Cedric White, who wore thick glasses, and saw that he had a sharpshooter medal on his uniform.

"Sharpshooter? Really? Boy, how you gonna be a sharpshooter and you can't even *see*? Raymond, don't ever go out in the battlefield with this boy. He liable to shoot one of his own. And teach him how to shine his shoes, too, because he can't see what a bad job he done."

No one said a word

"At ease, gentlemen, and have a nice day."

As Momma walked out, looking quite satisfied, she turned around to me.

"Raymond, you want dinner rolls or cornbread for dinner?"

She winked at me and walked down the hall, singin' Bill Withers' "Lean on Me."

Sergeant Parker was blown away by Momma's character and bewildered by her military knowledge. It must have been refreshing for him to have a Black person visit him at a predominately White school. He chased Momma down the hall.

"Ma'am!"

"Brother, I ain't that much older than you for you to be calling me Ma'am."

"How do you know so much about reading military stripes? Your old man in the military? I don't see a ring on your finger."

"My late husband was a Sergeant Major in the Marines, so I recognize the stripes. And no, he wasn't White."

Knowing that he wondered why I was so White, Momma left him with a classic anecdote that only Lemell Studevent could deliver.

"Sergeant Parker, ask yourself, if a brown cow eats green grass and gives off white milk, why can't a brown woman eat collard greens and give off a milky white son?"

Sergeant Parker was dumbfounded.

"Have a nice day, Sir."

13

"Once they find out you don't have the right zip code, they will kick your milky white butt right out."

I was not cut out for the rigid lifestyle of military school. Momma was extremely proud and believed that Calvin was smiling down on me from heaven, but his military legacy cast a large shadow and I felt tremendous pressure to excel academically and as a military cadet. Even though I maintained a 3.0 GPA, I came to the grim realization that I wasn't military material, but I was too terrified to tell Momma because I knew it would break her heart.

One day, she and I got into it.

"Momma, that school is a different world, and I don't fit in."

"Negro, do you realize how many Black children in this neighborhood would die to have this opportunity? I am killing myself to pay for you to have a good education! Now stop whining like a sissy. Nobody cares if you're Black or White! In the real world, the only color that matters is green—as in money!"

She couldn't understand my thinking.

"Boy, you got my blood pressure up two hundred over a hundred! Child, please!"

Like a typical self-centered teenager, I quickly responded.

"Momma, I am tired of being a sideshow for them folks. Some weird white Negro with a genetic defect gone awry. And yes, I said 'awry,' so your hard-earned money is not a total waste. Learned some new words with them folks!"

I had momentarily forgotten who I was talking to and she quickly set me straight.

"Oh, I see what this about. Watch your tone with me. You have been around them White kids too much. They can talk that way to their mothers, but I will put your head through that window if you don't come to your senses."

After we both calmed down, she took a breath to settle her nerves.

"What do you mean, you don't fit in? Evidently, you're fitting in because you made the honor roll. I was so proud to see your name in the school newsletter next to all those rich White kids. I pinned it up in my office for everyone to see."

"I'm a fraud, Momma."

"Raymond, you got medals pinned all over your uniform. What do you mean, fraud? You're a military man! Calvin would be so disappointed in you for quitting!"

Calvin had been dead for nearly a decade so that didn't resonate like Momma hoped.

"Momma, I appreciate all you've done, scratching and scraping and making it possible for me to attend such a great high school. I am not a military man. I can't live up to Daddy's image. Every day, I see pictures of him in his military uniform. I'm not him! I am Raymond, a white nigga trying to fit in with somebody! Somewhere! Anywhere! I hate it! I am too hyper. I can't focus! To be honest, all of these fancy medals for marksmanship were not even earned. I couldn't even hold the rifle still long enough to be a great shooter."

"Well, I can believe that from all those drugs your mother took."

"Hmm, really? Momma, you taking it there?"

"So, if you not a military man, how did you get those medals? Tell me you didn't steal them!"

Tears began to well up in my eyes.

"No, I went a week without eating lunch and paid the kid responsible for issuing medals. I couldn't take the pressure of living up to Calvin no more. It's not me, Momma! I'm sorry. I cheated in biology and these medals were bought. The pressure was immense."

"The pressure was what?"

I couldn't help but chuckle.

"Another one of my new White words."

Momma laughed.

"I know the word 'immense.' I just wanted to hear my private school money talking. Hmm, well, Son, it took an immense heart for you to share your feelings with me."

"Are you disappointed because I want to transfer?"

"As long as you go to another private school that I can afford I won't feel as though my money was wasted for two years."

Momma agreed that I could transfer to Archbishop Carroll High School. It was a less prestigious private school and was probably 95 percent Black. Although I was somewhat excited to leave St. John's, part of me felt like a failure.

During my last few months there, I was introduced to a world I never knew existed, and I cultivated feelings of resentment toward everyone, including Momma. I carried them to my new school and soon came to realize the source of my anger. They didn't come from prejudiced White students, teachers, or even parents. For the most part, the school was full of young men trying to fight through the normal trials of adolescence.

At St. John's, I developed friendships with students from other private schools, such as Gonzaga, Sidwell Friends, Georgetown Prep, and St. Albans. This triggered a strange inner rage. It wasn't like I was introduced to a secret White supremacist group or some clandestine society for the wealthy. I became jealous and envious of affluent Black students, especially those who came from a stable and loving two-parent household.

In my neighborhood, many, if not most children were raised by single mothers, but these rich, elite Black kids had two parents and seemed so happy. Spending time around them made me sad and stirred up emotions I could not explain or control.

I was constantly reminded that I was an abandoned child, an orphan his parents did not want. You don't know what you're missing until you see it first-hand. I was introduced to a community known as The Gold Coast, the upper northwest section of DC, where many affluent Black folks lived.

They didn't party like we did on the other side of town, but it was refreshing to be around bright, articulate Black teens. I was ashamed of how I spoke and how White students looked down on inarticulate Black kids. I purposely tried to improve my vocabulary and how I spoke. Back in my neighborhood, I had to "slang it up" to maintain credibility and not be perceived as trying to be White. With my pale complexion, that was always a concern with Black folks. Incidentally, my inarticulation saved me from many fights because Black guys would recognize that I talked just like them.

I got to know several fascinating, rich, light-skinned Black kids, and many of them used "the Second" after their last names, which I found odd. Momma had a simple explanation.

"Boy, that ain't nothing but a fancy, high yellow, Negro word for 'junior.'"

"In that case, from this moment forward, I would like all Negroes to address me as Raymond, the Second."

While I made fun of those "White-talking colored folks from uptown," I was growing envious of them. They were confident and not ashamed of being Black. I was certain they were interested in dating White girls, but I was mistaken. Their attention and allegiance were reserved for Black girls.

Momma appeared slightly tickled by this, and I thought she would be proud that I connected with some elite young Blacks, but her tone became venomous when she spoke about the way they treated Southern Blacks or country Negros.

"They think they are better than us. The only reason they let you into their inner circle is because of your complexion. Once they find out you don't have the right zip code, they will kick your milky white butt right out."

These families belonged to elite Black social clubs, such as The Links and Jack and Jill.

They appeared elegant and classy in every aspect of their lives and held prestigious formal galas, known as Debutante Balls. Learning about these led to an awkward conversation that nearly blew my cover. One day, inside the Gonzaga gymnasium, a young kid referred to himself as a "beau" and I wasted no time exposing my ignorance.

"Oh, easy to remember. I have a couple aces named Bo. Is that your nickname, Brotha?"

My clueless, ghetto mind thought he meant Bo, the name of one of my best friends. I thought it was his nickname. He was referring to himself as the young man escorting the girl who was known as a *debutante.*

Part of me felt proud to know these folks, but I was so jealous of them and soon realized that Momma was right. I learned the meaning of a word I had never heard—pedigree—a word common Black folk knew as "roots."

The elite class of Black people had a saying, a famous quote of Maya Angelou, which summed up the importance of family lineage.

"If you don't know where you come from, you don't know where you're going."

One car ride and a dinner invitation changed everything. I joined some of my "friends" at a football game where Jesse Jackson's son Jesse Jr., aka Jesse the Second, was a star running back for a prestigious school.

After the game, the parents of one of my friends from Sidwell offered me a ride to the subway. Both of them were light-skinned, which didn't surprise me at all. It was my first time in a brand-new Mercedes Benz S-Class sedan, which was like no other car I had ever been in.

"So, Raymond," the mother said, "what is your last name?"

"Studevent, ma'am."

"Do we know any Studevents, Dear?"

"That's Dutch, correct?" her husband said.

Afraid to embarrass myself, I quickly responded.

"I believe so."

The only Dutch I knew was Double-Dutch jump roping.

"Wait a minute," the man said. "The Virginia and Carolina Funeral Home Studevents?"

"That's correct, Sir."

I knew our relatives owned funeral homes in North Carolina, but I never thought it would earn me a pass with these uppity folks. I played it up like I knew all about our family fortune.

As the conversation proceeded, I dug myself into an eventual grave.

"Raymond, do you have siblings?"

"Yes ma'am, my oldest sister just graduated from Howard with a master's degree and my next oldest sister actually works at Howard."

I was checking all the elite Negro boxes.

"Did they pledge a sorority?"

My next answer garnered me an invitation to my friend's mansion for dinner.

"Yes, they are AKA, pink and green to the heart."

AKA is the sorority normally associated with light-skinned Black women.

"Well, Raymond, next Saturday at dusk we are having a few friends over to celebrate the firm's recent amalgamation. We would like you to come and have dinner with us."

I had absolutely no idea what dusk or a firm was, let alone what "amalgamation" meant.

While I was flattered that these rich folks considered me worthy enough to invite to dinner, my jealousy and resentment reared their ugly heads. I couldn't wait to get home and tell Momma about how that couple interacted so nicely, like she and Calvin used to do.

I teased Momma that some uptown Black folks had invited Raymond Stude-vont the Second, of the Carolina Stude-vonts, to a posh evening amongst the noble Negroes. We had a good laugh about it until she told me she didn't want to accompany me.

"Come on Momma, you're always talking about rich White folks never inviting Black folks. Well, here are some rich Black folks inviting us to dinner!"

Momma finally agreed to go. The evening turned out to be unforgettable and helped me understand Momma on a much deeper level.

We went shopping for something to wear on what promised to be a French-style evening. She bought me a black, double-breasted suit by Yves Saint Laurent and treated herself to an elegant, black, full-length Christian Dior dress.

Momma seemed excited but guarded, and the closer the day came the quieter she became. While I was painfully jealous of the affluent Black class, for one evening, I would be one of the "Carolina Stude-vonts," even if I belonged by default.

We arrived in class because Momma had recently bought a new Cadillac Eldorado. I was about to embrace the moment for a few laughs if nothing else.

I introduced myself to the valet.

"Raymond Stude-vont the Second, of the Carolinian Stude-vonts! Accompanied by my dear Madame Lemell Stude-vont."

Momma was not amused and seemed uncharacteristically nervous. We entered the foyer and after introducing Momma to my friend's mother, I left her to mingle while I joined Andrew in his "wing" of the mansion, along with a few of his other wealthy friends.

Things took an immediate turn after we sat down for dinner. Since it was a business celebration of some kind, each person introduced themselves. By this time, I realized that "amalgamation" meant merger.

Then it came time to introduce myself.

"Raymond Studevent, and I am a student friend of Andrew."

I had been hoping to avoid revealing that I went to Carroll, as it was looked down upon by these folks as a glorified public school, but I had to.

"Carroll, *hmm*," said Andrew's mother.

As she waved her hand slightly, the brilliant reflection of her enormous wedding stone nearly blinded us.

"I thought you attended Sidwell or St. Albans."

"Sorry to disappoint you, but I don't."

"Well, how do you know Andrew?"

"Mom," Andrew said, "I know him from St. John's, where he went before."

Momma introduced herself next.

"Lemell Studevent, Raymond's mother."

As usual, everyone stared in bewilderment.

"Lemell," said Andrew's father. "That's an unusual name. Where are you from, North Carolina?"

"No, I am not from North Carolina."

"Lemell?" Andrew's mother said. "I hope I pronounced that correctly. You have a fine son here, and Andrew tells us that Raymond serves soup to the homeless every Sunday."

I jumped in, afraid that Momma's blood pressure might spike.

"Momma always taught me to live by the Golden Rule."

Andrew's mother didn't miss the chance to display her wit or her pearly white teeth.

"Well, we certainly agree with the words of the good Lord. As you can see, we have been blessed. However, we Browns have adopted a more contemporary, more Goldman Sach-ish version of the Golden Rule, as in, 'The one with the gold, rules.'"

Confident in her brilliance, Andrew's mother clasped her freshly manicured hands together and clarified the gap between the uppity Negroes of DC's Gold Coast and us two niggas from the "plantation" side of town.

"Now, shall we convene at the refectory?" she said.

Momma and I had no idea what she meant. In fact, I had never seen Momma so withdrawn and overwhelmed by the moment.

Could she be ashamed of her Mississippi roots?

"So Lemell," a guest said, "where did you go to school and pledge? I suppose you didn't pledge AKA, being a bit brown and all. Nowadays, pink-and-green allows all shades to pledge. I mean on both sides of the brown-paper bag."

Fearing that Momma would let these high yellow Negroes have a piece of her mind, I spoke up for her. I was already jealous, but now I was angry. I put my arm around Momma and proceeded to do what she had done for me so many times. I came to her rescue.

"I know y'all good Negroes are trying to figure out what this is all about. Well, let me tell you so you can relax. This woman, my momma, is from a place called Crystal Springs, Mississippi. My real mother is a drug addict and my father, a Black man with a complexion rather common in this home, is an alcoholic and never cared much for me. This woman right here rescued me from an orphanage. Soon after, her husband died, and she was left with a decision. Take me back to a foster home, an orphanage, or try to find one of my parents. She decided that even though I was not her blood nephew, she would still adopt me as her own. She is the most amazing woman in this room, and I don't mean that to minimize the certainly impressive accomplishments of any other women here, but I seriously doubt if any of you hifalutin colored folks can top that. Andrew, did I use that word correctly, hifalutin?"

"I think so."

Momma smiled.

"Thank you son. Now, let's go."

We got up from the table and left without saying much of anything.

I broke the ice on our way home.

"Momma, now I know why you didn't want to go. I am sorry that those folks looked down on you. You will always be my hero and I meant every single word I said back there. Hey, I'm hungry Lemell. 'That's a rather strange name, ma'am. Lemell.'"

She giggled.

"I am feeling hifalutin myself," she said. "Can you pull into the McDonald's drive-thru?"

I thought of all those deadbeat dads trying to impress their kids with a Big Mac and felt so fortunate to have such a beautiful mother.

Momma and I grew even closer after that evening.

14

"Raymond, if you don't have God in your life, you're headed for the cemetery or prison or both."

After putting Momma to sleep with more stories, I fell asleep on the floor and woke up with an aching back and a growling stomach. McDonald's was open for breakfast, so I left the nursing home, wondering if Momma would remember any of *Butch Cassidy and the Sundance Kid*. Although Paul Newman and his mesmerizing blue eyes did not get a rise out of her, I hoped that some of our most tender moments from the past, which I shared, had some effect.

Linda called before I reached her house.

"Hey, Boy, are you okay?"

"Yeah, why?"

Apparently, the home director had called her, concerned about me and how sad I looked leaving the premises that morning.

"Come take a shower," Linda said, "and then let's take a ride down the 95 Freeway."

"How long a ride you talking?"

"You know what I'm talking about. You owe me a long-overdue explanation from thirty years ago."

"A full tanker?"

"Maybe two!"

When I was younger and Linda wanted to help me get back in line, we'd take long rides together. We classified these ride-along therapy sessions by their level of seriousness. A small issue was a "quarter tanker," meaning that was how much gas would be needed to solve the problem. With that in mind, I filled up the tank because I knew we had a long ride ahead.

I was hoping to avoid one of those therapy-on-wheels sessions ever since I started dealing with Momma's situation. Linda always loved a challenge and takes great pride in being able to diagnose people's issues and get them to see a solution. She became famous for inviting people for one of her "therapeutic rides."

We headed south on the freeway.

"So, Sister Shrink Studevent, what do you want to know?"

"Look, Boy, you know how this works, I ask the questions. I used to be a parole officer, so I am an expert interrogator and I'll know if you're lying or hiding painful details. Besides, I'm your sister and we are too old for that."

"Painful details? It's all painful, no details needed."

"Scoot, I spent nearly ten years in college and have been practicing this psycho mumbo jumbo thing for nearly forty. I was motivated after seeing what you went through with your mother. I have yet to figure out what went wrong in your life after Mom and Dad provided you with a safe and healthy environment. I know you, Raymond Lorenzo Studevent, and I know Lemell Studevent. So, let's have it.

What happened between that honor roll student with such a bright future and that strong Southern Black woman who you bonded with like none of us?"

I let out a big breath.

"The tank is full, and I want dialogue. I don't care if we end up in Miami!"

"One condition. Don't interrupt by asking me to go down side roads. Let me tell it as it mattered to me."

Linda agreed.

"The first thing that went wrong between me and Momma is that I told her the whole church-and-God thing was a farce."

Linda reneged on her promise and interrupted.

"What? You told a devout Southern Baptist Black woman that you had a problem with the Lord?"

"Just kick back and listen."

Linda nodded.

"I entered my senior year in a deep depression. I wasn't the same after leaving military school and I could also feel Momma's disappointment. She had high hopes for me to succeed Calvin as the military man of the house. As my classmates announced where they were going to college, my resentment and jealousy began to gain steam. I was actually accepted to Morehouse, but I didn't care. I had no interest in going down South and we considered anything below Northern Virginia to be Klan country. My friends were dropping like flies. Junebug got shot in the head six times in front of the house. While his mother Ms. Lee and his sisters were falling apart at the funeral, the reverend said, 'The Lord needed our dear brother to help him in heaven.' A few months later, Glenn Johnson was shot in the face four times and killed. A different pastor said, 'Our dear Brother Johnson was called for a greater duty to perform in heaven. Let's thank Jesus for the gift of seventeen years of life for our dear brother. Everybody look up and smile into the heavens, because Glenn is looking down right now at you, smiling.'"

Linda shook her head.

"Then D. D., my friend from next door, jumped out of a window and killed himself and his six-month-old baby. Lawrence Ellerbe got killed by a conveyer belt at the airport. Dennis died of AIDS. Ron-Ron was shot to death at Popeye's because he wouldn't give some guy his box of chicken. And don't get me started on the eleven-year-old Manning girl that was raped and murdered right out back. Hmm, God, whatever. Momma said they were in a better place and the Lord needed another beautiful angel in heaven. I went ballistic about God looking down at all these screaming Black mothers dropping their sons' casket into the ground. Then, the pastor of our church got exposed as gay! He was married with four kids and his wife caught him in bed with a man. Two days earlier, his sermon was about homosexuals burning in hell!"

Linda didn't say a word.

"So, I go to graduate college, work forty years, retire at sixty-five if I'm lucky, move to Florida, play cards and golf until I get cancer and die? If I'm good, I get a pair of wings and float around with all my dead friends. If I'm bad, I burn forever! Come on!"

"What did Momma say?"

"'The Lord works in mysterious ways and neither you or me can question his plans.'"

Linda nodded, as if she'd heard that answer before.

"I said, when your twin brother and husband died in the same week and your father a few months later, were you okay with that?

You never thought to question why God did that to you? 'Listen to me boy,' Momma said, 'no son, nephew, or anyone else will ever sleep in my house and disrespect the Lord. Raymond, if you don't have God in your life, you're headed for the cemetery or prison or both.'"

"Can I ask a quickie?" Linda said. "When was this, and did you move out?"

"This began toward the end of my senior year. The tension was getting thick. I wasn't going to the Baptist church anymore, but I attended the Seventh Day Adventist Church. Momma didn't like it, but she knew I was dealing with the deaths of my friends and she wanted me in somebody's church. She thought I had lost my mind when I revealed to her that I had found true religion with Jehovah's Witnesses. I told her that it made so much sense that God, whose name is Jehovah, would restore the earth back to a paradise and that we would live forever. I told her that Calvin would be resurrected and live forever on earth. She jokingly said, 'Tell your Jehovah's Witnesses not to come knocking on my door so early in the morning.'"

Linda laughed.

"I spiraled into a deep emotional darkness. My friends were getting ready to go to college and have the time of their lives. One day, I was at a carnival, talking to a good-looking girl, who turned out to be my cousin from my biological mother's side. I asked her, 'Why did Jackie never come see me? Sharon defended her. 'She wanted to see you, but...' I cut her off. '*Psst,* I was a bus ride away. She had no excuses.' 'Raymond, your mother is no longer on drugs and she moved to Pennsylvania. She wanted to see you before she left, but she thought you didn't want to.' The more Sharon defended her, the more irritated I got. I screamed, 'Why would she think that?' She said, 'Because you never wrote her back after she wrote you for years! That's why! You ignored her letters, and I know she wrote them because I helped her while she was in rehab. You live on 3819 Blaine Street, right? Ask that light-skinned nigga who lives next door. He tried to get my number. He saw me ask your aunt if she was Lemell. I handed her one of the letters and told her it was from Jackie. One time, I dropped it in your mail slot to make sure you got it. She wanted her baby boy to know that his mother was off drugs and wanted to see him as soon as she got better.' Sharon started crying. 'She was ashamed. She cried, telling me, your sister and the counselors at the rehab center that my son hates me and never wants to see me again!' I was so confused. 'I never got one single letter. I'm sorry, where is she now?' Sharon shook her head. 'Pennsylvania. She went to live with her sister, but nobody knows where she is now. I promise you, Raymond, she wrote you at least twenty-five times and it broke her heart that you never wrote back. It was one of the reasons she couldn't get clean.'"

"You're kidding!" Linda said. "Don't say what I think you are about to say."

"I was furious. I got Sharon's phone number. I was already badly depressed and didn't want to send myself over the edge, knowing Momma had kept Jackie's letters from me all those years, especially since she repeatedly spoke about Jackie not caring about me."

"What did you do?"

"I mailed a letter addressed to me and wrote Jackie's name on the return address. I wrote one sentence inside: 'Momma, it's not polite to read other people's mail and it's even worse not to give it to them after you've read it.' When Momma picked up the mail, I pretended to be asleep. I listened as she tore open the letter. I became anxious. I had never called Momma out like that. The disrespect I showed could have gotten me sent packing, but I was too sad to care. I had

contemplated suicide weeks earlier so this episode was just more reason to not trust anyone."

Linda did not move.

"I heard Momma shuffling through her drawers and talking to
herself. When she does that, fireworks are sure to follow. Her anger,
along with my inner rage and depression, set the stage for all-out war.
The moment was so tense it made me recall that only a few months
earlier Marvin Gaye's father had shot and killed Marvin for disre-
specting him. Momma owned a gun, and I knew she was old school."

"Did you really think Momma would shoot you?"

"I wasn't sure. I knew she'd kill me before she let me disrespect
her, especially after all the sacrifices she had made for me. She had a
special nerve that got triggered whenever the subject of Jackie came
up. There was no way she'd tolerate me defending the woman whose
neglect thrust me into the situation in the first place. And a blue-eyed
White woman to boot."

"So, what happened next?"

"Momma opened the door and in a deep and frightening baritone
voice I had never heard, she said, 'Negro, you ain't asleep so stop fak-
ing it. Look at me when I'm talking to you. I was taught as a little girl
to never trust a person with blue eyes, cause they ain't no good. I left
them devils in Mississippi and figured that the blue-eyed hate was just
a Southern thing. But your so-called mother, and all them whiteys
over there wasn't no different. Now I look at you, a nigga with blue
eyes, and you ain't no better. You are ungrateful and pathetic, just like
your sorry namesake and that pitiful White woman who gave birth
to you. It breaks my heart to say that about my own son and I never
thought I could go there with you because you suffered so much as a
child. But you're eighteen now; you're a man, so I'm going to address

you like one. I spent all that money for you to get a decent education and you got the nerve to not go to college and then disrespect me by sending me some smart-aleck letter. You left here for a few months to live with your father and didn't stand up for me then. One of that White woman's letters said she was off drugs, so I thought she might get some crazy idea like your foolish father and come snatch you away from me.' I said, 'She has a name, Momma. Her name is Jackie, not cracker, not White woman, but Jackie. And you know you're wrong, Momma. We both know it, even that God you always talking about, he knows it, too. So, when White folks call us Niggers, is God okay with that the same way you call my mother *whitey*?' Momma ignored my question and proceeded to unload on me. 'You're hanging with the Jackson boys and your ghetto cousins. Son, you will be dead in less than a year. What a waste. You're sleeping with all these girls and thinking you're not going to get one pregnant or get a disease. Don't you bring no babies around here.' I said, 'I don't care Momma. I hate everything and everybody. I'm not evil, just depressed.' "

"She didn't want to hear it, right?"

"Yeah. 'Please don't talk to me about no depression nonsense,' she said. 'Everybody has problems and I handed you a golden ticket to success and now you talk about being sad. I will gladly give you the letters from your mother. You can take them with you when you move out by the end of the month. By the way, leave that navy-blue suit I bought you for graduation. I like that suit and I am going to bury you in that one. Don't worry about leaving the shoes; the bottom half of the casket is never open.' "

Linda's jaw dropped a little.

"Momma said, 'You think those blue eyes and that White skin will get you through this world? You have no education and without that you won't be anything but dead or in jail.' 'Okay,' I said, 'let's talk about my White skin and blue eyes, which I love. For nearly fifteen years, I've fought just about every day on these crazy streets. See these broken fingers I got fighting Black folks? They are the reason why I couldn't learn to play guitar. Racist Black folks, who didn't even know I was one of them, did this to me. Your beloved Negroes hated me so much, I am going to leave you with them. I ain't playing Spades anymore. Time to play the joker, who is always a White man. Don't try to find me because I will change my name and embrace my whiteness. I won't go to prison; I won't end up dead. After all, I'm White, Momma. They don't send White guys to jail. I'm going to see what this world is all about. If I do die or go to prison, thank you for all you did for this little white Negro. You won't have to wait 'til the end of the month. I am leaving today to go conquer the White man's world disguised as a White man. I will put in a good word for the Negroes, okay." Momma said, 'My gosh Raymond, what has happened to you? You've turned into a monster. The rage from your childhood has finally come out. I saw it in your eyes when you stabbed that Thompson boy after Calvin died and I hoped love would conquer it. If you don't control your temper, Son, it's gonna cost you your life. It will serve you well in prison. I am tempted to go get my pistol and shoot you for your outright disrespect, but it shows me that you've lost your mind and my greatest fear has come true.' I told her I knew she had a pistol and if she pointed it at me, I wouldn't blink. I said, 'I am tired of this Black-and-White curse, tired of my contaminated and drug-infected brain that never shuts off.' Momma left and came back with a shoebox of letters. She threw it so the letters spilled all over the place. 'I suggest you read them before you go to jail,' she said. 'Leave my keys on the table and God bless you, Son, you're going to need it.'"

"What did you do?"

"As I gathered up the letters, I noticed they'd been opened and read. I was angry and a little excited because this was evidence that my real mother actually cared about me. I was hurting so much because I knew I had caused Momma terrible pain. But I could not make sense of why I was going crazy. Momma stood in the hallway, filing her nails, which was a clear indication that she'd had enough of the ungrateful li'l blue-eyed Negro. 'You're such a disappointment,' she whispered, just loud enough for me to hear. She was not done. She sliced me right to the core with her final words. 'Raymond, you know why people like your Momma do drugs? They are too weak to handle the tough challenges in life. People like your father hide behind alcoholism because they ain't strong enough to look life in the eyes and punch back when it hits them with a hard blow. They're quitters. You quit St. John's, you quit pursuing college, and so you are now blaming some racial identity crisis and your parents. You're a quitter and a coward just like your weak mother and father. I guess I'm not surprised because you're the product of two cowards so it's in your blood.' Man, nothing cuts to the core of a man when his own mother calls him a coward and a quitter."

Linda shook her head.

"Momma stood outside as I packed my stuff in the car. I gave her the house keys and told her I'd give her back the garage key after I removed some of my things. She predicted I would get a girl pregnant, go to prison, and die by the time I was twenty-five. Well, we were about to find out if she was a prophetess. Sadly, one of her prophecies came true within six months."

Linda was dumbfounded.

"That would explain why you guys didn't speak for the next four years!"

"Do you want to hear more?"

"Of course!"

We kept driving.

"So, the only thing that brought me a bit of calm was studying the Bible with Jehovah's Witnesses. I liked what I was learning, but I was too twisted emotionally to preach to folks about the new truths I had learned. I was nineteen and knew I had lost control of my life. I moved into a friend's house and the first night I read Jackie's letters. A few weeks later, I ran into two former classmates who thought I had gone to Morehouse in Atlanta. I felt so dejected, telling them I had decided to stay home until I knew what I wanted to do. They were excited to see me and show me their dorm rooms at Howard. As soon as we walked in, I felt a wave of emotion and began to feel sick—not because I wanted to go to college. I just realized how much I had disappointed Momma. I remember seeing the pain in her eyes when I told her I had no interest in college and didn't care if she had wasted her money sending me to private high school. Then I felt even worse when I heard about some of our classmates and how great they were doing at Virginia Union and UNC and Boston College. Little did they know, while they were all killing it, I was ready to kill myself by jumping off the dorm room balcony."

"You're on a roll, Brother. Keep going."

"After seeing my friends so happy, I fell into a deep despair. I wasn't obsessed with college. I simply couldn't handle not being wanted by my parents and I was still dealing with the race issue. My brain never shut off about that. I was lost. I heard Momma's voice loud and clear, telling me I'm a coward and a monster. I had to agree. Momma was right, that the monster always dies in the end, and I was ready to make the ultimate coward move and commit suicide. Add me to the list of sad deaths in Momma's life!"

"Raymond!" Linda shouted.

"Then I began to get religious. I thought, okay, the Jehovah's Witnesses taught me that the Bible says when we die, we don't go anywhere. But all those years in the Baptist church and Catholic military academy taught me that most decent folks go to heaven. I never believed in the heaven and hell teaching, so that night, after hearing all the success stories of my friends, I was going to finally settle the issue. I was crying, walking across the Howard University campus, talking out loud and losing my mind. 'Yeah, whatever Momma,' I was saying. 'I hear you telling me, I told you so. I am going to show you how much pain I'm in and that it's time to check out.' I spent that night deciding whether to join my friends and lead a life of crime or to check out and end my life. In the midst of that madness, all I heard was Momma, telling me I was a quitter."

As we drove on, I rolled down the window to get a little air.

"Sis, I began thinking about our cousin Richard and Mr. Robinson, who both put a gun to their heads and ended it. All the madness I had experienced finally caught up to me. I felt like they were in a better place, not heaven, but asleep, as I had read with Jehovah's Witnesses. I thought it's time for old Scooter to take a long nap. Girl, I was tired. No parents, no race and no future and a warped feeling of no love. It was time to check out. I drove from Howard to Momma's house that evening and pulled my car into the garage. I still had the key. I decided to die from carbon monoxide poisoning and left Momma a note."

"What did you say?"

"I haven't forgotten a word of it. I said, 'Momma, I quit, but thanks for everything. If I see Calvin, I will tell him you said hello.' The moment of truth had arrived. All I had to do was turn the key and I would never see another sunrise. I leaned back against the headrest and started laughing and crying at the same time. I thought, this is absolutely ridiculous, and then I heard someone opening the small side door. It was Momma, and she wasn't happy. She signaled for me to get out of the car. 'Back already?' she said. 'I guess your blue eyes and pale skin didn't quite work out, huh? What's it been, three weeks?' I apologized to her for the things I had said.She mistakenly thought I was asking to come home and I repeated my apology, that she didn't deserve what I said even though she had hidden those letters. True to form, Momma went in for the kill. You know how she always felt underappreciated?"

Linda nodded.

"So she says, 'let me get my point into that hard head of yours before I start looking for your casket.' She was keeping her voice down; afraid the neighbors might hear her. 'Young man,' she said, 'remember how you screamed when you first came to visit us? Look at your chewed-up fingernails if you don't. Remember how you screamed when you heard police sirens, when they scraped the skin off of your legs from the pot pie that burned your skin down to the white meat. Everyone heard you from inside the ambulance. Look at your lip and feel the back of your head. I held you in my arms to quiet your screams. This nappy country girl from Mississippi did all that.' I didn't know what to say, other than to remind her that I knew all that. Then she noticed the hose in the tail pipe. 'Are you going to do that to me, to us, after all I have done for you and all the death I've endured? You going to leave me a lasting memory of killing yourself in my garage?'"

I relaxed my grip on the steering wheel.

"Momma wrapped her arms around me. I cried and thanked her for stopping all my screams. 'You have been amazing to me,' I said. She wiped my tears. 'So, this is how you repay me, by having them roll your body out of here under a sheet?' I collapsed on the floor. 'What is it, Raymond?' she said. 'You got this crazy Black-and-White curse, as you call it. I know your friends been murdered and you didn't go to college. Those rich, uppity Black folks got you down again? What is it?' It took me a minute, Linda. Momma got irritated. 'I'll give you something new to scream about if you don't open up that wounded heart and tell me what happened to my little blue-eyed devil? Okay, that's a bad word; how about *rascal*, the boy who wore his Pierre Cardin suit to match the Yves Saint Laurent I couldn't afford, but we dressed up sharp for church. Where is *that* Raymond?'

"I had to tell her. 'He died in that church, Momma. You stopped all my screams except one. Remember on July 4, 1974, when I asked you if Daddy was okay? You and the family dropped your heads and said nothing, and I ran off crying and screaming. Remember? Momma, the man who rescued me dropped dead and my screaming only stopped on the outside. I've never recovered from Daddy's death. That's why I wanted to kill myself. Not to hurt you but to end the screaming.'

"Momma seemed shocked, 'Cookie was in a state of shock for four years,' she said, 'so I guess I understand.'

"I continued 'Listen, Momma, I may die, go to prison, and have a bunch of illegitimate children, but I won't care. And please don't get me any psycho mumbo jumbo doctors.' She asked me for the garage keys and what I was going to do. 'First, here are your keys,' I said. 'Then, I am going out into this world and prove you wrong.' She looked sad and disappointed. 'No matter what you do,' she said, 'please don't ever put drugs in your body.' 'Momma,' I told her, 'I was born on drugs and that's probably why I am so crazy.'"

Linda looked at me warmly and I kept going.

"Momma couldn't resist a final shot. 'That White woman, I mean Jackie, probably passed so many drugs down that you would fail a drug test right now.' I shrugged my shoulders and blew out a breath. 'Whatever, Momma,' I said, 'let me go see what this world is like through the sad blue eyes of a Black man trapped in a White body. I'm sure you don't see it as a trap, but maybe a blessing to be cloaked in pale. I remember that phrase, 'cloaked in pale face,' from one of the books you gave me. Don't worry Momma, you raised me to be strong. Bye.'"

"You left? Just like that?"

"Momma stood with her head down and arms folded. I felt bad but my sadness overrode any compassion. As I started backing out of the garage, I said, 'Momma, this is not your fault.' I must have offended her because she got sarcastic and said, '*Psst!* Boy, please, I know it's not my fault. You are just a fool, Nigga. And never forget you are one.' 'I am a what? A fool?' She said real firm, 'Don't ever forget that no matter where you go, you're still a Nigga. And don't think White folks won't detect that you're as Black as the shadow you cast, Negro.'

"I wanted the last word, so I said, 'Momma you always say, 'Wit' the Lord there is always a light at the end of the tunnel,' she said.

"Yeah, but the light at the end of the Devil's tunnel is a train."

"Then she turned and walked into the house. As I drove off, I had redemption on my mind. One way or another, I was going to prove Momma wrong. I didn't need to go to college to be a success and there was no way I'd go to jail. But I didn't say I wouldn't break the law. I simply thought like most criminals do, that I was way too smart to get caught."

15

"Which suit do you want me to bury you in?"

A s Linda and I drove in silence for a few minutes, I watched her digest my story.

"Are you following me, Miss Famous DMV Therapist? Is it coming together for you?"

"It's coming together slowly. But still there are some missing gaps."

"I promise to tell you more, but I'm hungry and in full 'Negro-mode. Aren't you hungry?"

"I can eat."

"Time to get Niggafied and hit Popeyes. Let's clog some arteries."

"Child, I haven't had Popeyes in years."

"Oh, that's right! Big-time therapist done moved up with the uppity colored folks. Now, it's poached eggs and broiled chicken, smothered in a cream sauce made from scratch."

"Yep, right out of a Campbell's soup can. Okay, let's get your lips greasy and do Popeyes. Then you make a U-turn and head back. I want to hear about why you and Momma didn't speak for four years. Jail, kids, all of that!"

After laughing our way through Popeyes, I gassed up the car and resumed my story.

"I wasn't a criminal at heart. All I wanted to do was prove Momma wrong, even by illegal means. It didn't take me long. One day, less than two months after that night in the garage, I ran into my old buddy, Boogie, who told me how much money he was making in what had become his chosen profession. We had friends working at car dealerships and Boogie paid them to steal vehicles off the lot. At that time, after the Mariel boat lift, Miami was a hotbed of activity for the drug trade. We drove the cars to Florida and sold them to some Cubans who used the engines for their racing boats. I had just seen *Scarface* and wanted to meet some real-life Cuban drug dealers."

"*Scarface*, Raymond? For real?"

I nodded.

"Boogie wanted me to drive because he figured we wouldn't get pulled over on account of me looking White. He followed me in a car with legit plates, so the highway patrol never got behind me to read my stolen plates. Boogie slept the whole way back to DC. I got $2,500 in cash and Boogie took his cut in cocaine, which he fried into crack rocks and made thousands. I'm telling you, Boogie was charismatic and made a life of crime seem exciting. He schooled me the entire night before our first run. He talked really low so no one in the adjacent hotel room could hear. I listened close because he had served time for bank robbery. 'Scoop, I will refer to you only as G. They don't need to know your name. Wear your shirt untucked over your waist to give the impression you have a gun. Most important, don't make any expressions. The Cubans like to soften you up with jokes but don't blink. Give them what we call dead eyes. That means you are so cold-blooded you have ice water in your veins. They smell fear and might try to take our cars if they think we can be had. Stay by the warehouse door while I work the deal.' Man, I couldn't sleep. The next night, when I was standing guard at the warehouse door, looking at real-life killers, I hear Momma's voice, saying 'Which suit do you want me to bury you in?'"

"How did you go from being an honor student to hanging with Cuban drug dealers?"

"Yeah, exactly what I was thinking. The next incident helped me see that the world of crime wasn't for me, certainly not violent crime, 'cause these guys were killers. One day, in the car with Boogie, I noticed two guys next to a phone booth. I lived there, so I knew that phone didn't work. My friends had crowbarred it open for the coins and damaged it. I told Boogie something wasn't right, and he accused me of being scared for no reason. As soon as we got out of the car, they started shooting at us. I ran, bullets whizzing by me, and barely escaped. Boogie jumped a wall and ran down an alley. When we met up, Boogie was laughing because he had been shot at numerous times and felt invincible. 'I sold some guys in Baltimore some fake crack.' Damn! Another incident with some friends of the notorious drug kingpin, Rayful Edmonds, convinced me that several people were looking for Boogie."

"You got lucky, Raymond."

"Not really. I was arrested with him and he had a gun. I got bailed out because Boogie and I had a stash of cash in his apartment. He had a girl get $10,000 to bail me out and we had no intention of show-ing up in court. With his enemies in DC and Baltimore, and now potential jail time, I figured my only recourse was to get out of town. I was scared and started seeing myself lying in a casket wearing my favorite blue suit."

"You mean to tell me being shot at wasn't enough to get you to come home?"

"No, they knew where I lived, which scared me enough to leave town. Boogie decided to move to Miami and become a drug runner for the Colombians. He had a contact in Los Angeles who would set me up with cars that I could sell to some Mexican drug dealers. He gave me a stack of brand-new birth certificates and some coffee-stained ones he slow-baked in the oven to make them look old and told me to see his friend with connections at the California Division of Motor Vehicles. My judgment was clouded by depression and desperation. I couldn't see a clear way out and didn't realize I was on a slow, self-destructive road to either death or prison."

Linda rolled her eyes.

"I got an adrenaline rush with this life of crime, and being a fugitive was exciting. Momma had no idea where I was, and I wanted to keep it that way. Boogie drove me to the airport on his way to Miami. We shook hands and said, 'Let's shock the world and become rich and famous.' As we took off, the pilot said, 'Folks, if you look outside the plane you can see Arlington National Cemetery.' This reminded me that I had failed to live up to expectations and that Calvin's legacy still haunted me. I remember thinking, *I don't care about the Studevent name or my failings. I'm starting a new life with a new name, in a new place and a new attitude.* While I tried to convince myself otherwise, I knew I was a failure. It tortured me, but I pretended not to care about anything or anyone. I arrived in Los Angeles and connected with Boogie's contacts. I had a pocket full of money, a bunch of new aliases, and a seemingly foolproof money-making scheme. My anger faded, and under the spell of beaches, glitz, and swaying palm trees, life was looking up. I wanted to find out what The Beach Boys were singing about, so I chased the famous California girls."

Linda rolled her eyes even more.

"I knew it was pure kamikaze, but I didn't care. For the first time in my life, I was not Black or White. I was free from the emotional shackles of that crippling issue. Best of all, I was no longer Raymond Studevent, because I had a glove compartment full of aliases and fake identification cards. Best of all, I didn't have to see the disappointment on Momma's face."

I picked a piece of Popeyes out of my teeth and flicked it out the window.

"Once I got settled, I had quite an operation going. I made contact with a security guard who agreed to provide me with wholesale birth certificates. I sold them to illegal immigrants from Mexico for $500 a pop after setting up my coffee-stain operation like Boogie. I also delivered pick-up trucks and Ford Broncos to Mexican drug dealers, who installed Mexican plates on them. When I heard that higher-ups in the drug world were looking to save money on expensive cars, I began delivering Mercedes-Benzes, BMWs, and other high-end cars to a pick-up man at the border. Life was sweet, and as I earned the Mexican gangsters' respect, they arranged for a guy to pretend that he had a problem with me to see if I was a punk. To prove my manhood and establish my domain, I beat the guy senseless. I had learned from the day my BB gun was taken from me to use my hands with ridiculous speed. It didn't hurt that the guy had a few shots of tequila in him. I had a really bad temper back then, so I hesitated to carry a gun. But I had gotten in too deep and reached a point of no return. Against my better judgment, I started carrying a pistol for emergencies and to promote the appearance of being one to fear."

"You?"

I nodded.

"I was nowhere near as ruthless as the Mexicans, but they always made me money and had a gorgeous gal waiting for me. They adopted me as a gringo ranchero and even gave me nicknames, such as The Güero Ranchero, The Don Juan of Culiacan, The Durango Chilango, and a host of other crazy ones I can't remember. Because my fictitious name was Italian, they also called me Eddie Spaghetti, Ragu Lou, and Macaroni Tony. These guys were ruthless, but they were also a bunch of clowns, the funniest guys I ever met. I laughed even when their jokes weren't funny for fear of losing my life. Mexican criminals had the most fun—music, dancing, and a bunch of gorgeous women. Lemell Studevent and everything else from the first twenty years of my life seemed like a hundred years ago. No one back home knew where I was because Raymond Studevent no longer existed. The only color that mattered to me was green, as in cash money. As long as I stayed busy, I was good. I wanted to go to bed exhausted so I wouldn't be reminded of my past. By then, I was delivering stolen cars from dealerships to the border. One day, I was set to deliver a Dodge truck to a farmer in Wasco, California. I parked at a phone booth to make arrangements and didn't realize I was in a no-parking zone. After I got off the phone and took off, an undercover policeman shined his red light on me. I was stunned and pulled over. Normally, I would have never made a rookie mistake like that, driving without a back-up. When he asked for paperwork, I pretended to reach for the glove compartment. Then, I did something stupid. I floored it. 'Come on copper!' I began racing through the outskirts of Lancaster, trying to shake the cop. I could hear sirens everywhere. I was in a full-on, high-speed chase. I heard a helicopter above me and hoped it meant I'd be featured on the news that night. I screeched to a halt in a parking lot, abandoned the Dodge, jumped a couple of walls, and hid in a

Dumpster. I pulled trash bags over me, but my $400 suede Fila jacket got caught on the outside. The second I heard dogs, I knew the party was over. A detective yelled out, 'Son, get out of that trash now! I have a .45 pointed at you and if you even budge, I will blow your head off.' "

Linda looked a little freaked.

"I crawled out and looked at the helicopter. 'Hey, I must be bigtime. Can you tell me what channel that chopper is from?' The detective snatched me by the collar. 'You nearly killed someone during the chase.' They threw the book at me, and I went into the Los Angeles County jail system under an alias. Those were the days before law enforcement caught up with fake driver's license scams. I was roughed up by the downtown deputies for risking the lives of their comrades. I said to myself, 'Momma, I guess you were right. Here I am in jail.' "

"You weren't dead yet and didn't have any kids."

"Not yet. I came to the grim realization that I was facing a new situation. Up until then, I only knew Black culture and I didn't talk like the whites in California. I was put in a cell with some of the meanest looking White and Mexican men you could imagine. In order to survive, I had to assert myself. I singled out a White cellmate who looked tough. I asked him if he knew me. Naturally, the guy replied that he didn't. 'Well, stop looking at me then,' I said, 'unless you wanna get your teef knocked out.' The problem was, I pronounced teeth with an "f" on the end. One of the White inmates caught that slip up. 'Hey, my man says he has a problem with you because you walk and talk like a nigger. You need to handle him, or we are going to handle you.' I caught a break because the guy had long hair. I grabbed it the way I used to see Black girls grab other girls' hair in fights and gain complete control. I smashed his face against the bars and threw him on the ground. 'Nigga, I will kill your cracker butt in here!' Those words

out of my mouth summed up my life. I realized I was both a nigger
and a cracker. It was clear that as long as I was willing to fight Black
inmates, I was going to be fine."

I heard Linda exhale as I concentrated on the road.

"During the months awaiting sentencing, I survived by referring
to my own people as niggers and a number of other racial epithets I
had never heard before, like knuckle-draggers, toads, spooks, coons,
and other crazy names. It was so surreal because I had only known
about the Klan and Southern racism, but now I was in Los Angeles—
the American West, a place with no Civil War history and all that
goes with that—incarcerated with haters of the highest order. Even
in jail, I thought about some things Momma told me. Her disdain
for White men with blue eyes hit me loud and clear. Behind bars,
there are basically three gangs that run each race. The Black Guerilla
Family, The Mexican Mafia, and The A.B., effectively known as the
Aryan Brotherhood. These are the craziest White dudes on the planet,
quick to end anybody's life, regardless of race. They were more likely
to kill or seriously maim one of their own quicker than a Mexican or
Black. One Aryan guy, named Gary, benched 500 pounds. I saw him
knock out three guys, each with one punch. He had the scariest blue
eyes. Fortunately, I had grown up in the streets of DC, so I was man
enough to fight anybody. I lost a few, but it didn't matter, because as
long as you weren't a coward, you earned people's respect."

"That's messed up."

"Yeah, but it's real. During my entire time in prison, I never con-
tacted anyone. I was too ashamed, and I knew Momma would have
been devastated. I never told her. I felt a sense of relief in prison
because everything is taken care of and there's no pressure to live up
to any expectations. Your only responsibility is to survive. I took some

scholastic aptitude tests and scored high in writing and math. The education and vocational trainers asked me to write an autobiography because they were fascinated by my story. Little did they know I lied about everything. I wrote two copies of a fictional autobiography so I could remember the details. During a parole board hearing, one officer became skeptical. He was Black, so I figured I would put my best Black voice on for him. It had been nearly two years, so I had almost forgotten how to talk like I used to. 'You know, son, something just doesn't add up.' he said. 'I read your autobiography. Your name is Italian; you talk Black; and you have the writing skills of a scholar. You study the Bible in here with Jehovah's Witnesses, of which I happen to be one. I hope you continue to study the Bible and apply what you learn. Otherwise, you will end up waiting for the resurrection, because you will end up dead. Yet, you were out here stealing cars for thrills."

Linda shook her head in disbelief.

"Fortunately, the parole board agreed to release me with a year remaining on my sentence, under the condition that I went to San Diego. I was banned from Los Angeles County until my parole was complete. I soon began thinking about how to resume my life of crime. I had not been rehabilitated whatsoever. During my two years in prison, I made new contacts and learned many new ways to beat the system so I couldn't wait to put them into action. I was a felon with a fake name and absolutely no idea who I was.

"No wonder Momma couldn't find you. She hired a private investigator, but you were three thousand miles away living under an alias with altered fingerprints. You must have been gone emotionally to do all that. Your abandonment issues left a deep scar within you."

As we sat in Linda's driveway, I nodded. She was right on the money.

16

"Boy, I actually loved you as one of my own as best as I could."

Several days later after our therapeutic joy ride, Momma's doctor asked Linda, Cookie and me to come to his office. We felt impending doom until the next day, when we gathered for breakfast and joked like old times.

"Raymond, I hear you bared your soul to Linda," Cookie said. "It's not fair that she gets to hear the whole soap opera. What about me?"

"Go on little brother," Linda said. "Tell Cookie about all the craziness."

"You girls really want to hear more?"

"Silly question. Course we do!"

"Okay, we have some time to kill, why not?"

"Lay it on me," said Cookie.

Linda didn't waste any time.

"Pick up right after the parole board approved your release."

I cleared my throat and slugged down some more coffee.

"Like most men who get out of prison, my first order of business in San Diego was finding a girl. I wasn't allowed to leave the country, but Tijuana was so close, and that's where I met Evelyn. I had promised the Jehovah's Witnesses that I would connect with them in San Diego, but I had an outstanding warrant and fines to pay and I was still using an alias. I noticed that my new parole officer didn't carry a gun and I told him that my sister was a P.O. and she carried one. 'I am one of Jehovah's Witnesses,' he said, 'and because we value life, I don't carry.' See? The Jehovah's Witnesses shadow was following me."

I watched Cookie and Linda eye each other.

"I was tempted to call Momma. I called the house a couple times, just to hear her voice, and then I hung up. No way I was telling her about prison. Her words were right so far and would soon prove prophetic again."

Two sets of eyebrows raised up.

"A few months later, Evelyn came to my house with her mother, who just stared at me with her arms folded. Evelyn was shy so she whispered, 'I am four months pregnant and you're the father.' We hadn't really been dating, and I didn't know how to respond. I heard Momma's prediction in my head and something a recent acquaintance had warned me about, that Mexican girls always try to get pregnant to get citizenship for them and their kid. 'No! No!' I said. 'You trying to trap me. I want a blood test, a DNA test! That baby is not mine!'"

More eyebrows.

"Evelyn's mother said, 'My daughter is not a whore; she doesn't sleep around like American gringo girls. That baby is yours and you will see because it will look like you.' For the next three months, I told her I wasn't taking care of the baby she claimed was mine. When Evelyn was about seven months pregnant, she stopped by my apartment. We were in the midst of an argument when two federal agents showed up with a warrant for my arrest for a crime I committed back in DC. Boogie and I had done so many things I had no clue what they were talking about. 'I am sorry,' I said to Evelyn, who just stood there crying. Turns out, Boogie had been murdered and their investigation tracked me down. They used my failure to appear on the gun possession charge as leverage to get me to give them information on who killed Boogie. I convinced them that I had no idea, but I had to go back to DC for the previous charge. My lawyer, Alex, put his law license on the line to guarantee that I would show up in court. He also put together a strong plea package for the judge. I didn't trust anyone in the criminal justice system, so I figured I was going back to prison."

I checked my watch and we still had time before seeing the doctor.

"I agonized for an entire month about seeing Momma. I didn't know if I could walk into her house as an ex-con, soon-to-be father, and a flat-out failure. The interrogation by the feds would seem like a job interview compared to the one I would get from Momma. Despite my trepidation, I knew it was cruel to leave her wondering if I was even alive. Alex assured me that if I showed remorse the judge would likely give me a fine and probation. I decided I'd better see Momma before Monday morning, just in case the judge was not in a good mood. But there was no way I could tell her the truth about that or Evelyn. I knew the baby was likely mine. I didn't care as much about standing before a federal judge as I did facing my real judge, Lemell Studevent. I had not spoken to her in nearly four years. I went to see Momma on Sunday, figuring she would be in a forgiving mood after church."

Cookie and Linda nodded at that notion.

"Remember, Cookie? You opened the door. I walked in the living room and Momma greeted me with her famous, 'Hey man!' After bringing her up to speed, she recited a long list of my neighborhood friends who had been murdered during my absence. Then she moved on to the success stories about friends who had graduated college. Although she was happy to see me, it didn't take long for her to unload on me for staying out of touch so long. 'I couldn't locate what jail you were in. They must have shipped you out of town like the White inmates. If they knew you were a nigga' I could have found you.' I told her I was working in Southern California, but not in jail. She wasn't buying it. 'Yeah, sure you didn't go to jail. I see you got a tan. You got a White girlfriend, too? Those blue eyes and white skin don't mean nothing without a college degree, do they?' I was holding back my tears. 'No, Momma, I learned that most White people aren't prejudiced and there are some nice ones with blue eyes.' She was having none of that. '*Psst,* that's because you're so dumb,' she said, 'and you don't realize they only act like that because they think you're one of them. Don't come back here with no White girl, trying to show off. I won't open the door.' It was as if she had rehearsed her lines because they rolled off her tongue like a machine gun. 'How many kids you got, Boy? Today is Sunday so you better not lie in my house.' I was absolutely devastated. Her anger and disappointment were clear. 'You've never had muscles like this or your fingers all twisted. I bet that comes from fighting in jail. Yeah, you're nothing but a two-bit liar who thinks I am some dumb Southern nigga' who don't know nothin'. I still got that blue suit upstairs to bury you in.' I was astonished that she saw my broken fingers and knew they were from fighting in jail. 'Momma, why are you so angry, I thought you would be glad to see me?' 'Glad to see you! Glad? Negro, you disappear for four years and expect me not to be worried sick. Despite what you might think, Boy, I actually loved you as one of my own as best as I could.' I tried to talk, but she yelled over me. 'I would rather you tell the truth, that you were in jail, at least that way I could understand not hearing from you. But you can wake up every day and not care enough to at least let me know you are alive.' Nothing! Four years! Nigga please!' I thought to tell her I had gone to jail but by that point she was too enraged."

Cookie had a pained look on her face, as she had overheard some of this exchange.

"As I made my way to leave, she wouldn't let up. 'Since you say you are living in California, why did you come back'? I just said, 'Listen, Momma, I don't have kids and I came by to say hello. It was good to see you. Next time, it won't take four years.' I had no intention of coming back any time soon. I would only return for redemption. The next day, to my delight and surprise, the judge let me off the hook with a fine and stern warning. He said, 'I cut you a break because your report says you are an expectant father and never had a father. Son, you need to break the family cycle. Now, if you decide not to be responsible, you better duck for cover because I'm telling the next judge to throw everything at you. Don't make a fool of me, Son.'"

On the flight home, I thought long and hard about the devastating effect Calvin's death had on all of us. I didn't want my child growing up without a father. I saw inmates not able to touch their children. It was so sad to see little girls asking their fathers when they were coming home. The judge was right, and Evelyn was telling the truth. When I got back to San Diego, I went to Evelyn's house and told her that I would help her raise our child."

Linda looked pleased to hear me say that.

Then what?" said Cookie.

"A few weeks later, December 1990, my baby girl was born, and Evelyn named her Gizelle. I was in the delivery room and when I held this beautiful tiny newborn in my arms, my heart just opened up. I hadn't expected such a rush of emotion. I had no idea what parental responsibility was all about. I got a job offer at a pest control company in Los Angeles that paid nearly double what I was making in San Diego. I wrestled with the idea of living a hundred miles from Gizelle, but I figured the extra money would mean more toys and gifts. Like I said, I was young and stupid."

"Can we agree with that?" Linda said.

"Keep going," said Cookie.

"It was another four years before I saw Momma. I wrote letters and called on her birthday and holidays. The disappointment in her voice always made me feel sad like a big loser. For a couple of years, I didn't tell Momma I had a daughter. But the more responsible I became, the more I saw fatherhood as an opportunity to redeem myself with her. I knew she wouldn't like it that Gizelle wasn't Black. Momma always loved how much I talked about beautiful Black girls. It gave her confidence that I would not date or certainly not marry a White woman. As Gizelle got older, I realized I was parenting like Momma in how I disciplined Gizelle to make her bed and wash the dishes and taught her how important it is to respect adults. I had no idea how to be a father because I only had limited memories of Calvin, but I did my best."

"He was the best, Raymond," Cookie said.

I smiled and nodded.

"I kept thinking, one day I'll introduce Gizelle to Momma. I was certain she would be proud of me for being a responsible father and I'd tell her how I learned from her example. This should earn me a measure of redemption. When Gizelle turned four, I finally got the courage to have Momma meet her youngest granddaughter. Momma was so sweet to Gizelle, and she was trying to seem proud of me. But the minute Gizelle was occupied, Momma began her onslaught. 'Why didn't you bring her mother?' I said she lives in San Diego. Momma put it together that I lived far away and was not shy about telling me that I wasn't the dependable father I purported to be. 'So, you go to Mexico,' she said, 'get a Mexican girl pregnant, and now you live in another city one hundred miles away from your Spanish-speaking daughter? Do you have any plans to have a stronger role in her life?'"

"Never good enough, right?"

"Hello?"

I shrugged at my sisters.

"Momma said, 'Nigga', I'm not stupid or impressed. I know your type. You live in Los Angeles so you can chase floozies. You need to live where your child is so you can be a responsible father.' At that point, I had no choice but to tell her that Gizelle's mother and I were no longer together. 'Of course not!' Momma said. 'You want to chase girls and risk getting AIDS instead of caring for your kids, and yeah, I said kids because I don't believe that the little Mexican girl is your only one.'"

This time, I rolled my eyes.

"I flew back to California with my tail tucked between my legs. Momma had a way of making me feel like a helpless, pathetic loser. While I hated what she said, I knew she was right. I should live in the same city as my daughter. After that, whenever I called, I made sure she knew Gizelle was with me and I hoped she would lighten up. It didn't last. I resumed my party life in Los Angeles. I'd even call home to make sure Momma knew I was having a blast in sunny Southern California. I would say things like, 'Yeah Momma, I am meeting mature women and making myself a desirable husband.' She only cared about me being a father. 'You need to move back to San Diego and take care of that little girl before you get another woman pregnant. Raymond, take care of that child of yours. She needs her father. That weekend stuff doesn't work.' That was the only concern she had."

"She was right, Raymond!" Linda said.

"Yeah, I know. I walked around angry for months because I knew she was right about so many things. I was so stupid to think I could fool Momma into believing I had made something respectable of myself. And the Black and White issue did not go away. The Rodney King riots and the O. J. Simpson trial put race relations on another level. My identity crisis was in full bloom, and it seemed like every day I had to give my opinion, which became exhausting because I knew if I didn't agree with Black folks I would be labeled a sell-out and if I didn't agree with White folks I was a sympathetic race traitor full of White guilt."

"Talk about being caught smack in the middle," said Linda.

"Yeah, I was one of those crazy fools screaming on the overpass, 'Run O. J. Run!' I called Momma to see if she watched the freeway chase and she said, 'Boy, you know that man didn't kill them two White folks. They just setting up another famous, good-looking brother because he married that White girl. Y'all niggas will learn someday about messing with White girls.' It was a horrible time. Made me want to do something more with my life. One night, in a comedy club, I noticed most of the comedians were talking about their insecurities. It was therapy for them. I knew I made folks crack up at my stories so I saw it as a challenge to see if I could convince a rambunctious Black crowd that I was actually half-Black."

Cookie and Linda looked at me in disbelief.

"Black folks can smell a fraud immediately, so I had like no wiggle room, especially with the racial climate in Los Angeles. I tried a small club first, called Maverick Flats on Crenshaw Boulevard in the heart of the ghetto. I bombed so bad the host interrupted my set, and I was laughed out of the place. I had never been so humiliated, but being from DC, I had a chip on my shoulder and I vowed that vengeance would be mine. I read a few autobiographies by comedians and turned my spare bedroom into a makeshift stage to practice. I went to friendlier clubs in the suburbs and after my fifth time, a manager at the L.A. Cabaret asked me if I could be that funny for an hour. He offered me a 10 PM slot on a Saturday, which was prime, and I lied and told him I'd be on the road for six weeks. I needed that time to prepare a full set. Turned out I did really well and proved I could headline a full hour. I couldn't wait to mail Momma a picture of me featured on the marquee. She loved comedy and I sent her a video of the performance, too. I couldn't wait to hear her response. 'Yeah, I got it a week ago,' she said, 'but I don't have a VHS player, so I gave it to your friend, Keith.' I said, 'Momma, you couldn't go to Cookie and Linda's house and watch it?' She laughed. 'Boy, I hope you didn't quit your job. Your cousins said you were funny, but you use profanity. I don't care to watch you cursing, I raised you in the church. Get funny without cursing and maybe I will watch.' I was furious, but she wouldn't let up. 'I hope you spending more time taking care of that little Spanish baby than trying to write jokes.' I said a quick goodbye and slammed the phone down. I performed a few more times around Los Angeles, but the grind was too hard, and I had a child. I proved to myself that I could headline so mission accomplished."

"Oh Lord," Cookie said. "What next?"

"At a Hollywood Boulevard party a model scout and agent handed me her card and asked if I had ever thought about modeling. I told her I always think about making money and getting girls. She promised me that modeling could do both, so I signed with her agency. I had to get used to gay photographers and agents. Many of the male models were bisexual, and some came on to me. Next thing I knew, I was on a greeting card wearing Lucky Brand jeans with "Feeling Lucky" on them. The more magazines I was in, the more excited I became. My Lucky Brand jeans poster went up in the fitness center I used, which led to free workout gear and drinks, and I bought a convertible Porsche to complete the picture. Still, though, I was always looking over my shoulder because I never forgot that I had crossed some guys in Los Angeles, and they hadn't forgotten. I waited until I had plenty of material to send Momma, and when I called, all she said was, 'Boy you look like a sissy, posing for those White folks. I hope you aren't gay. Calvin would roll over in his grave if he saw these pictures.' Momma advised me not to show them to anybody because they might think she raised a sissy. I was angry and didn't care if I disrespected her. I laughed and said, 'Momma I get paid six hundred dollars an hour and you're making fun of me. I make in one day what you make in a month.' She lashed back. 'Yeah, but I can sleep at night, knowing I have a respectable career. You have no idea what it means to be a real man like Calvin. At your age, he was fighting in Korea and you in tight drawers, posing like a wimp.' I knew modeling wasn't a career. I was worried that someone from my criminal past might recognize me and seek revenge. I was never comfortable in that superficial environment either. I gave it up. I couldn't escape this cycle of feeling like a sad, lost soul. You wouldn't think it to look at me, driving around Los Angeles in a convertible, but I was thinking of suicide again."

"What stopped you from doing that?" Cookie said.

"Gizelle. If I didn't have her in my life, I may have succumbed to the pain. I used to drive up and down the Pacific Coast Highway with my tears drying in the wind. Although I was twenty-eight by then, I had no foundation, no roots whatsoever. I was so lonely. I had the car, the body, the magazine photos, and for a guy in L.A., that was the dream. For me, it became a nightmare. I was treated like someone special there, but Momma thought I was nothing but a white Negro, trying to integrate myself into a White world. Achieving redemption weighed so heavy on my mind it became an obsession, and it led me back to more trouble in Miami."

"What did you do?" said Linda.

I took a long drink of water and looked at my watch.

"Girls, you realize we need to get a move on."

Cookie protested.

"Oh no! You can't stop with a cliffhanger. We need to know what happened in Miami."

"I have a few things to do before we go to the Alzheimer's facility. Miami has to wait for another day and time."

Cookie objected.

"You better believe we're going to keep talking about this. There ain't no way I'm going to let you off the hook, White boy."

17

"If you give a man without a college education a million dollars, he will go broke in five years."

As soon as Cookie and Linda realized that we had to wait to see Momma's doctor, they were on me to continue my story.

"Don't leave out the juicy stuff," said Cookie, "or enhance it to make you look good."

"So here's the truth, the whole truth, and nothing but the truth. I'm one of Jehovah's Witnesses so I can't lie. I was bored with Los Angeles and wanted a change, but no way I could leave Gizelle behind. Then I got set up on a date with a wealthy woman from Miami who was looking for a nice man. We hit it off, and after a few months jetting back and forth, Michelle asked me to move to Miami and live with her. She had made a great deal of money in the stock market and agreed to help me to do the same. 'Don't you want money to pay for your daughter's college tuition?' she said. The legit money was appealing, but I couldn't leave Gizelle."

Linda nodded.

"Remember Yolanda, my sister, whose mother was Connie Christmas? Linda, you are the greatest shrink I know, but Yolanda is brilliant in helping people get beyond anything shallow and superficial, whether it makes them look good or bad. She wrestled with me on my decision to move to Miami. 'If it doesn't work out, you can always come back,' she said. 'However, don't come back until you get that redemption from Lemell.' In my mind, that meant kick butt in the stock market and make serious money.' Miami, the City of Redemption, here I come. I went to stock market seminars with Michelle. I practically lived at a country club where Venus and Serena trained. I worked out with millionaires and they called me the California Kid and welcomed me into their inner circle where I picked their brains about investments. They invited me on their boats and to exclusive parties. DC and L.A. seemed a million miles away. Michelle's work ethic was incredible and contagious. Momma's lessons paid dividends, too. She used to say, 'Never let the next man outwork you. Work smarter, not only harder.' Michelle patiently explained everything. Over the next few years, we visited the Chicago Board of Options Exchange and the New York Stock Exchange, where she met with young hotshots and handed each of them brand new Rolexes and a check for $10,000. Michelle told them that she wanted prompt execution of her trades or she'd take her business elsewhere. She even paid a man $100,000 to sit in her house one time and let us watch him execute trades. I realized I was playing with the big boys. I loved staying at the Waldorf, eating $100 steak dinners, and sitting in first class. I kept thinking, if Momma could see me now, and redemption time was drawing near. I flew Gizelle to Miami and spent tons of money on her. I had missed her, but once I started making all that money I hid my feelings of regret by mailing her a few dollars and tickets to see whatever boy band she wanted. 'Lemell Studevent, get ready, 'cause your baby boy is loaded and ready to shut you and everyone else up.' That became my mantra."

More eye-rolling from my sisters, but plenty of curiosity.

"Momma had no idea that the new Ray and his millionaire girl-friend were heading up I-95. Michelle wanted to fly, but I told her we could enjoy the long road trip. My real reason was to drive her $100,000 Mercedes straight to Momma's front door. I made sure Michelle would make it clear to Momma that I wasn't some young boy toy she liked to parade around the club, even though she was seen as the millionaire cougar with the young hotshot boyfriend. She was seventeen years older, but we had an incredible connection based on a mutual desire to hustle and make money. I only cared about what Lemell Studevent thought about her son's success. Michelle agreed to say that I was her primary research analyst even though I was too inexperienced for her to trust me with millions of dollars. I did make real money in my own account, though. My $80,000 doubled and tripled and I was full of myself. Michelle had a chip on her shoulder, too, because the White male-dominated world of finance didn't give her the respect she deserved. So, we were kindred spirits."

"Guess we know who's paying for dinner tonight," said Cookie.

"Keep talking," Linda said.

"Okay, so the night before we left, I waxed the car with a special $1,500 product I ordered from Germany. I was so excited I made Michelle bring her mink and silver fox coat because I wanted to make a huge impression. When we arrived, some of the neighborhood guys checked out the car. I rushed Michelle inside the house because people will rob their own mother inside the church on Easter Sunday for wearing a coat like she had on. Momma greeted Michelle and me with big hugs as she caught a glimpse of the Mercedes. Then she noticed that Michelle was way older than me. 'So, Michelle, do you have children?' she said. 'How old are they?' That was her way of getting Michelle to reveal her age and to make it clear that her makeup wasn't working. Michelle recognized Momma's intent and politely said both of her children were in college. 'Yeah,' Momma said, 'must be nice having your kids go to college, but this one here never learned.' Michelle jumped in like she was playing Double Dutch. 'Well, I used to believe that,' she said, 'but I never went to college and retired at thirty-nine. Raymond is so smart that if he keeps working like he is, he'll retire at thirty-five.' Momma didn't buy it, suggesting I wouldn't stick around long enough for that, and then Michelle, loving the verbal volley, snapped right back, telling Momma that she hoped to make life sweet enough for me to stick around. 'And if Raymond does leave,' she said, 'I'll make sure he walks away a rich man.' Momma said, 'We will see, but if you give a man without a college education a million dollars, he will go broke in five years.' Michelle smiled. 'With all due respect Mrs. Studevent,' which Momma interrupted, saying, 'Excuse me, you can refer to me as Lemell, Sweetheart, because you're closer to my age than his.' Momma was on a mission to keep everything between us ice cold, so I tried to warm it up. 'Momma, Michelle is training me in the stock market.' 'Training you?' Momma said. Who are you, the Karate Kid and she's that old Japanese man?'"

Linda and Cookie had a good laugh.

"Michelle said, 'Raymond has told me that he regrets not going to college, mostly because he feels he disappointed you.' I thought, bingo! Game, set, match! Let the redemption begin! After hearing Michelle defend me like that, I could have married her right on the spot. Momma, however, was just getting warmed up. She said to Michelle, 'So, Ma'am, did this boy tell you he is Black? Because you looked a bit surprised when you walked into my house today.' Michelle said I told her I was Black, but considered myself White with Black blood in my veins.' Momma went upstairs for a second and came back with her ace in the hole, my birth certificate, which she shoved in front of Michelle's face and said, 'Lady, you see what it says? Black. Don't say nothing about White folks. Did you tell your family that this child is Black?' For the first time ever, I saw Michelle flustered. Before she could respond, Momma went for the jugular. 'Of course you didn't tell them,' she said. 'And there's no way you will tell your daughter or your parents that you're living an immoral life laying up with some nigga half your age!' All Michelle could say was that she never thought about it. I whispered to her that we could leave and drive up to New York. Michelle said, 'Raymond, in the Asian culture we always show the utmost respect for our parents. Your mother has a right to speak her mind in her house.' Being the ungrateful American I was, I said, 'Well, I am not Asian and, in this country, when you are grown and on your own, and your parents are wrong, they can get unloaded on just like anybody else. Momma walked slowly down the stairs. The only time she moved slowly is when she held a cigarette and lighter in her hands while holding the railing. In full gangster mode, Momma did her signature, 'I just smoked you' move. She lit up a cigarette and purposely blew her first big puff in the direction of Michelle's mink coat, which was on the couch. This was a woman known on Wall Street as one of the 'Big Dogs,' recognized as the second-largest options trader in the country, earning six hundred thousand dollars a month, who could garner standing ovations from a roomful of millionaires. In a matter of minutes, Lemell Studevent, who made less than thirty thousand dollars a year, had reduced this hot-shot millionaire to a sad puppy like you see on late-night TV, staring ahead, looking for a home."

"Your dream of redemption just died," said Linda.

"You said it. Michelle was humiliated and I figured I was next. We went to dinner that evening, knowing that an epic verbal showdown was brewing. I don't think Momma spoke another word to Michelle. She was waiting to speak with me in private. When the valet went to get our car and Michelle was in the bathroom, Momma said, 'Boy, what in the world are you doing with this old, rich Chinese lady? You done went to Miami and got with a Chinese Golden Girl.' I said, 'At least she's not White!' 'Close enough! said Momma. 'She ain't nothin' but a banana, yellow outside and white underneath. In my book, she's White. Can't you find a Black woman your age? You need to go back to California and raise your Mexican girl so she has a father in her life. Chinese women! Mexican babies who don't speak English! What's next, an Indian with a red dot on her head? Boy please, you're like the United Nations.' I was irritated.

I said, 'She is forty-seven, and Vietnamese, not Chinese!' Momma didn't miss a beat. 'She eats rice with chopsticks, right? Vietnamese, Chinese, Japanese; you enjoy your fortune cookie while it lasts and take that money and go to college.' I asked Michelle to wait by the door so I could unload on Momma. 'Linda went to college, got more degrees than a thermometer, and probably makes $100,000 a year. I made that last week on one trade! She is probably still paying back student loans!' "

I paused to see how Linda and Cookie were reacting. They loved to hear about Momma being "Momma."

"Keep talking," Cookie said.

Linda nodded.

"Once again, I had failed to earn Momma's respect. I expected her to be proud of me and at least acknowledge my financial success. She wasn't impressed. In fact, she seemed insulted. I looked petty and cheap, not classy and elegant. Michelle told me I shouldn't have showed off all those pricey material things. The anger I felt made me more determined than ever to make even more money. With Michelle coaching me, I made hundreds of thousands and had a lavish lifestyle, but I wasn't happy. In my delusional mind, I decided I could force Momma to accept my success, as if I could buy my redemption. She was accepting the money and gifts I sent. I once rented a stretch limo for her birthday and took her shopping and for lunch on the waterfront. She softened up a bit after I sent her on vacation to Hawaii."

"But no redemption," said Cookie.

I shook my head. Linda waved me on.

"After four years living in the lap of luxury, I was depressed. Every time Michelle sensed I was feeling down, we would buy a new car, but that never helped me overcome Momma's lack of respect for me as a man, and I missed Gizelle tremendously. I saw her every three or four months, but like the old saying goes, 'A father's presence is more important than his presents.' I was falling apart because I knew I should help raise her. Then the stock market took a nosedive. Michelle and I had problems because I was withdrawing from her and she suspected I was cheating but I wasn't. I just didn't care anymore. I was so depressed I didn't want to talk, eat, or get out of bed. I was ready to die. The only emotion I could feel was regret that I had lost Gizelle's college savings in the market. I had failed to increase her chance of escaping the deadbeat barrio she and Evelyn were living in. I just wanted to go home and raise my daughter and forget about proving to Momma that I had become a respectable member of society. After nearly five years, I had learned that money does not guarantee happiness and my faint hope of achieving redemption with Momma was on life support. She taught us that when life becomes too much to handle, we need to lift our heads and pray to the Lord to help us. In a last-ditch effort one day to avoid another suicide attempt, I reached up from behind my desk, where I was curled up in the fetal position, pulled out a Bible and poured my heart out in prayer. That was my last hope. I called a Jehovah's Witnesses friend in Los Angeles and he said a woman he knew had moved to Miami and would help me. I had met Flynn before (she'd been married to Richard Pryor), and we rekindled our friendship. She grew up in DC, not far from us and she was mixed-race, too. She told me that the only way to overcome my depression was to study the Bible and allow Jehovah to guide me. I'd paid lip service to going down the right path, but I'd never committed to it, which kept me in the same self-destructive cycle. Even worse, I'd caused other people pain and heartache because of my actions. I was finally ready to find a measure of peace and purpose. I started getting my spiritual house in order and studied the Bible with Flynn's husband, Rico. This gave me a better perspective so the decision to move back to San Diego became a lot easier to make. I needed to get my financial house in order, too—through legitimate means—so I asked Michelle to help me resolve some of my financial obligations, which she did. I cringe when I think about how much money my depression cost me, but the value of having peace of mind with God, along with a wonderful father-daughter relationship, which Gizelle and I developed, is priceless."

I took a deep breath and continued. Linda and Cookie urged me on.

"After so many different lives—as an orphan, a White boy, a Black boy, a military cadet, a playboy, a criminal, a model, a stand-up comedian, and living briefly as a millionaire—I finally found my purpose. I decided to be a Christian, knocking on doors and spreading the Gospel, and a father to Gizelle who was present and reliable. I only had about $25,000, but I didn't care. I had grown to despise the stress of chasing money. While I was sad that I lost Gizelle's college savings, she was only eleven, so I still could find a way to get her a degree. As I drove from Miami to San Diego, I had a lot of time to think about Momma, too, the one person whose approval I still needed. How would my newfound love for the Bible sit with her? In the Black community, there was tremendous respect for the Bible, but when someone made it their sole focus it was often viewed as a cop-out and a frivolous excuse for not doing more in the real world. Becoming one of Jehovah's Witnesses was going to make Momma and most of my friends and family think I had gone bonkers. Momma, especially, was going to think I lost my mind. But I hoped she'd respect my decision to move back to San Diego and become a responsible father and God-fearing man, maybe even enough to get me some measure of that illusive redemption."

"So what happened in San Diego?"

"I felt relief waking up without the stock-market bell. I trusted that my faith would provide me with a fresh start. Fortunately, I got a job with the pest control company I had worked for ten years earlier. That was lucky because a normal background check disqualified me for most everything else."

Just then, the three of us got called in to see Momma's doctor. Sadly, it turned out to be just as we feared. Her Alzheimer's had worsened to Stage 7, the final one of the disease. At this stage, most people cannot speak and need help with most activities because they also lose psychomotor capabilities.

It was a difficult meeting. The doctor said Momma's health was relatively good, and she could live another few years. Some patients with advanced Alzheimer's have lived for up to twenty years. Obviously, the quality of life during Stage 7 would be seriously compromised. Linda, Cookie, and I discussed this information and decided to bring Momma home so she could be around family and friends. They needed to run tests before releasing her to us, which would take a couple of days, giving us time to make arrangements for Momma's homecoming.

As you grow older, you realize that you need to be grateful for every moment. I knew I appreciated my two amazing sisters, first for all they did to embrace me as a kid, then to listen to all my stories, and now to take on the burden of caring for our beloved Momma.

18

"If you are truly my son, and you want me to believe this stuff you been telling me, then take me home and change my diaper!"

When move-out day for Momma came, she had no idea we were bringing her home for good. She thought Linda, Cookie, and I were taking her to lunch. My sisters stepped up tremendously by volunteering to take care of Momma, Cookie during the week and Linda on the weekends. Since I was flying back to California, they let me spend most of the day with Momma, so I began with a ride to Arlington National Cemetery where Calvin was buried.

It was a long shot that all those tombstones would trigger something in Momma's memory, just as Paul Newman's blue eyes had failed to do. Still, I was excited that Momma trusted me enough to ride together in the car. Just a few months earlier, she thought I was a strange "White, honkey, cracker," trying to assault her.

"Momma, any songs you'd like to hear? How about some O'Jays?"

"O'Jays? O'Jays? O. J. Simpson, sings now?"

That response confirmed the doctor's diagnosis. Momma was confusing situations and people. I played one of her favorite O'Jays tunes, "Use ta Be My Girl" and a medley of songs she used to love.

As we entered the cemetery, I turned off the music.

"Is this where my husband is buried?"

"Yeah, I thought it would be nice to visit the man who brought you and me together. I haven't been here in quite a while."

I pointed up the hill.

"That's where JFK is buried."

Momma looked baffled.

"Who is JFK?"

"Well, some Black folks would say he was the best president the United States ever had, other than this guy named Lincoln."

"JFK huh? Blue eyes?"

Not knowing exactly the best way to answer, I played it safe.

"No, his eyes were not blue."

"Well that explains why he was a great man to Black people," said Momma.

As we walked toward Calvin's tombstone, she gently grabbed my hand for balance.

"I see on that tombstone it says "Spouse." Does that mean I will be buried here, too?"

"It sure does, Momma. You will be placed right on top of him."

She chuckled and pointed.

"You mean my body will someday be right here? How can that be if I am going to join him in heaven? I know he's up there because I would have never married a man who didn't love the Lord."

We stood in silence for a bit.

"Hmm, so this is Calvin's resting place."

The saddest time in both of our lives was the day of Calvin's funeral and his burial at Arlington. Now, forty-four years later, as we stood in that same spot, Momma pulled out her Bible from her purse and handed it to me.

"Young man, look at me. You are holding the word of the Almighty God in your hands. Remember, if you lie, you're in a cemetery so God can drop you right where you're standing. Now, as you stand before me, Calvin, and God, do you absolutely promise that you are my son?"

"Absolutely."

Momma turned to look at the tombstone.

"Okay, can you give me a moment so I can talk to my husband in private?"

I walked away but stayed close enough to hear her say a prayer, apologizing to Calvin for not remembering what he meant to her. The last part I still remember.

"I am standing here with your nephew. Calvin, if you are looking down, I hope that blue-eyed rascal isn't making a fool out of this old Black woman. I hope I did you proud by raising this boy. He may have lost his way for a bit but that wasn't my fault. Maybe it was his drug-addicted mother. I know my end is near, Darling, and I am coming to join you soon. I promise I will remember who you are in heaven. God, thank you for sending this crazy young man back into my life. Sounds like this old Black woman did okay. Amen!"

When Momma finished, she exhaled, turned around, and shuffled a few steps to me.

"First of all, Son, didn't I teach you that it's rude to eavesdrop on folks' prayers? I want to thank you for helping me realize that my life had some sort of good and purpose. I am confident that I can stand before the Lord on Judgement Day and feel that I've pleased Him."

I couldn't resist joking with her.

"Well, Jesus might be looking at you with those blue eyes of his. Is that okay?"

"I've gotten enough practice with my son, so I'll be fine. And yes, you do have beautiful blue eyes, but don't stare at me too long."

We laughed and Momma grabbed my hand as we headed back to the car.

"You're not tearing up on me, are you Boy? I know I didn't raise you to be a softie."

She elbowed me in the ribs.

"If you are truly my son, and you want me to believe this stuff you been telling me, then take me home and change my diaper!"

Of all places, Arlington National Cemetery was where Momma finally accepted me as best as she could. I took her home and shared more stories that made her feel good about all she had accomplished. Two days later, I headed home with the acceptance I had desired for so long. As I read the information Momma's doctor had given me, I thought of her happy reaction to me becoming a full-time father to Gizelle. It brought me great pleasure to tell Momma about Gizelle earning an athletic scholarship and graduating from The Bishop's School, the most prestigious high school in San Diego, where the tuition was nearly thirty thousand dollars a year. When I told Momma that Gizelle had earned a full-ride scholarship to Penn State University, she really warmed up and seemed as proud of me as she was of her granddaughter.

While visiting Gizelle during her freshman year, I spent a few days in DC and saved my visit with Momma for last. At a café in

Georgetown, she gave me a moment I will cherish forever. I was proud of Gizelle and my role in her success, but much to my chagrin, Momma didn't waste any time throwing shade over the situation.

"Gizelle got a full ride to Penn State. What was her GPA?"

"She went to the most difficult high school in the county, Momma."

"So, isn't she one of these impressive athletes who are also great students? Would you say she's more of a dumb student but a gifted athlete?"

"Momma, she graduated with a 3.8 GPA. I know, I know. She couldn't pull off a 4.0."

Momma flashed a smile I hadn't seen in years.

"Now, I can tell all my friends at the women's club that my granddaughter got a full-ride basketball scholarship. They are always talking about their little over-achievers so now it will be my turn."

"Momma, if it weren't for all those lessons you gave me on studying hard and staying focused, Gizelle would have never learned the importance of an education. I know I didn't listen to you, but sometimes we learn more about ourselves through our failures than our successes."

She then opened up in a way I never expected, especially since her brain was failing.

"Raymond, I know I was really hard on you. And I was disappointed in you as well. However, let me tell you how I feel now, since you have grown into manhood. To my knowledge, you have never done drugs or drank alcohol. I think these two wise decisions are the reasons you're still alive. I am proud of that, especially considering your mother and father."

"Momma, you always reminded us of the destructive nature of anything that alters our thinking."

"I know that the Black-and-White issue has been hard for you. Every single day, you have to accept that you are not what you appear to be. I would hate to have such a curse. Being from Mississippi, I had a tough time with White people, and you know how blue eyes spooked me as a child. I was unfairly harsh on you during your younger years and I should have realized that you had gone through enough trauma by the age of five than most people experience their entire lives. For that, I am sorry. I should've recognized that between the trauma and the racial dynamic you had to deal with, I was insensitive. I am sorry for treating you like that."

I was dumbfounded. Utterly speechless. I was afraid her clarity might disappear at any second and that she might even stop recognizing me.

"Momma, I wasn't the easiest kid to raise so you deserve a medal for your patience."

"I totally understand why you had to leave and find yourself. It wasn't just me keeping your mother's letters from you. I was afraid she was going to take you away from me."

I laughed.

"I'm sure there were times you wished she would've."

We shared a good laugh about that.

"You were just hyper, and the drugs in your system contributed to that. I'm proud you became a door-knocker. Becoming one of Jehovah's Witnesses was the best thing that happened to you. I may not understand their teachings, but ever since you started going to their church, you have matured to a level I never imagined. You don't use profanity; you lost that crazy temper; you stopped chasing women, and you seem happier than you were when you were rich."

I nodded. She had hit it perfectly.

"Having God in your life can never be a bad thing. But don't start preaching to me now. Y'all Jehovahs always want to get into a Bible discussion. I told you before; I agree that I saw God's name is Jehovah in my Bible, but that's all I can give you now."

"I'm good with that, Momma."

"Son, when you drove back to California and left Connie Chung in Miami, I was proud of you. You took on the challenge of fatherhood. Calvin died too young for you to understand what fatherhood is all about."

"Momma, I just had to remember how sad Cookie was after he died. It all turned out okay. Thanks Momma, this means a lot. But I have to ask you something. Why did you take care of me after Calvin died? You didn't have to, so why?"

Momma took a sip of her coffee.

"Raymond, sometimes God presents you with an opportunity to make a difference in someone's life. I didn't do what I did for you because I loved you. I did it because *God* loved you. He just used me to demonstrate that love. The Lord knew I had a problem. You needed to be loved and I needed to be taught a lesson. You made something of yourself and I no longer have an issue with blue-eyed folks. Well, almost."

I sat there digesting her profound words.

"Son, if circumstances arise, asking you to be there for someone in their time of need, and you know you can make a real difference, please, by all means, do it."

I nodded, not knowing how prophetic her words would become.

"I am so proud of the young man you've become. Who would have thought that an ex-convict would not drink, do drugs, not curse, be a Jehovah, and on top of that have a daughter go to a great school on a full-ride scholarship?"

"What do you mean, ex-con? I never told you I went to prison."

Momma raised her eyebrows and laughed.

"Boy, you didn't have to tell me. I'm not stupid."

"I was in Mexico trying to find myself."

Momma winked.

"Sure you were, *Amigo*."

That day at the Casino Café in Georgetown gave me the acceptance and redemption I needed, and it brought us closer together. While Momma never bought my lie about being in Mexico instead of prison, my trip to Mexico produced Gizelle and could there ever be a better blessing than that?

As I touched down in San Diego, I was at peace. Life was good. Little did I know, it wouldn't stay that way much longer.

19

"I'm proud of you, Son."

Three days later, I woke to the sound of rain pelting against my window. As I made coffee, I thought of Momma, who always had a strong cup to start her day. I normally don't drink coffee on weekdays, but for some reason I wanted some that day. My thoughts of Momma were interrupted when my phone rang. Linda never called so early.

Please, don't let this be the call.

I let it ring once more and took a deep breath.

"Don't say it. Please, Linda, don't."

"She's gone."

"I knew it, Momma! I knew it!"

"Boy, don't you see? Momma held on as long as she could. Aren't you glad you two had that final conversation at the cemetery?"

I agreed with Linda, but I had to hang up. I stood motionless, numb and helpless because the woman who saved me was dead, just when we were in a good place. I couldn't accept that this invincible woman who had sacrificed so much was gone.

Linda called back but I didn't answer. I texted her that I needed time to pull myself together. I laid on my bed, staring at the ceiling as the tears flowed. I asked God for strength to accept this brutal reality. The Bible teaches us that those who die will be resurrected, but even Jesus cried when Lazarus died.

Momma left this world the same way she came into it, with absolutely no idea who she was or why she was here. We all go, but watching a loved one deteriorate so fast is brutal. This woman gave her heart, mind, and soul for those she loved and ended up reduced to a lifeless corpse, tossed into a freezer drawer like a bag of vegetables.

This was my early stage of grief. I was desperate to blame someone or something, but she was eighty-eight years old. Still, you can't prepare for the abrupt finality death brings, especially when it comes to your mother. My heroine was gone, and there was nothing I could do.

Heroine. Sounds just like heroin. One rescued me from the other. Momma was my personal 911, saving me from a miserable childhood.

A few hours later, I snapped out of my downward spiral, which had left me feeling like a fifty-two-year-old, broken-down mess. At least Momma had died at home, warm in her bed.

I once read in a medical journal that people hold on until the last of their children come back into their lives. God had made the stars align for us, and I was thankful for that. But soon enough, I thought of the moment I dreaded most: Momma's funeral and my role as her only son.

It was up to me to make sure that everyone attending knew that Lemell Studevent was an incredible woman. I needed to man up and orchestrate Momma's final goodbye with the grace and dignity she deserved. This would be my chance to share what she meant to me. But first, I needed to cry a river, and I did!

As the day drew near, I felt more and more anxiety. How many stories should I tell, and would I have enough time to give Momma her due? I wrote my eulogy during the cross-country flight while one of my favorite movies, *Titanic,* played on a laptop next to me. That ship sailed on April 10, 1912. Lemell Studevent was born on April 10, 1930. The vessel was made from tons of black steel, and yet it broke in half and sunk. Momma was made from Southern Black Mississippi steel and didn't sink. They both set sail on the same day, but the Titanic only lasted a few days while Momma persevered almost ninety years.

Eventually, I chose five stories starring Momma and her blue-eyed Negro son. It was therapeutic reflecting on the great and not-so-great times we shared, but those feelings quickly dissipated when I realized we were landing. Instead of staying with Linda or Cookie, two strong women who have never needed the support of a man, I chose a hotel to prepare for the funeral. Momma's wake was the following day with just the three of us.

We met at Stewart's Funeral Home. My sisters were calm, mostly concerned that Momma looked good for her viewing. They told the director that the casket was wrong, and I used the confusion to avoid going near it. But I couldn't keep stalling, and as I neared it the reality hit me. It was just as my sister had said on the phone.

"She is gone."

As they adjusted Momma's hands and the pearls around her neck, all I cared about was keeping it together. Nothing had prepared me for the sight of Momma lying in a box that would soon be placed beneath the earth. She seemed at peace, but I wasn't. This would be the last time we'd see Momma.

The next morning, I made my hotel bed in memory of Momma, who told me to make my bed every day. As I ate my breakfast alone, I held her funeral program with a picture of a young and beautiful Lemell Studevent.

At Momma's house, we piled into limousines and headed to the church. I put on a happy face, and while I appreciated everyone being there, all I could think of was not disappointing my sisters, or Momma, with my good-bye speech. As I heard the choir, my palms began to sweat.

The time came for the immediate family to be escorted to the front row. The entire congregation was Black, so many of them wondered who I was. To my surprise, they had already closed the casket. I remembered Linda telling me that it would be too emotional for us to have the casket open. Black folks are notorious for losing themselves in an emotional stupor at funerals, especially as the casket closes while the choir sings at a fever pitch. Momma's casket was so close. If I wanted, all I had to do was reach out and touch it.

The choir nearly blew the doors off and the swaying and clapping got everyone out of their seats as the energy became electric. Halfway through the program, I couldn't stop crying. Linda did her best to console me because the family was depending on me to deliver a speech. Momma was revered by everyone who spoke.

Then it came time for the blue-eyed, white Negro to stand before a jam-packed Baptist church in the ghetto and share his account of the Black woman who saved his life.

"Next, we will hear from Lemell's son, Raymond Studevent," the reverend said.

"Here we go, Momma," I whispered.

I am Lemell's son, and for those of you here who don't know me, I can see that look of disbelief on y'all's faces. You must be thinking, "I know Lemell's husband was light-skinned, but this is uncanny." I'll get to that. Let me set the stage. Momma was born in 1930, in Crystal Springs, Mississippi. Now, these streets of DC are rough, but there isn't a person here who would have rather grown up in segregated Mississippi during that time. We were taught that slavery was over by then, but Momma picked cotton for so little money it may as well been for free. The woman in this casket could not drink from the same water fountain as any White woman here. But she held her head high and kept pushing toward something better. And Momma did it with style and class.

For those of you not here for the viewing this morning, trust me, my sisters and I made sure that Momma was clean and looking good.

In 1974, Momma's brother died. We all went down to Mississippi. A week after his funeral, while still in Mississippi mourning that death, her husband collapsed and died of a massive heat stroke. Later that year, her father died. Just a few months later, Linda, her oldest daughter, got hit by a drunk driver and broke her back and legs. She rolled across the stage in a wheelchair to receive her college diploma. During this time, Momma had to repeatedly chase burglars from inside our house. When she christened her newly purchased .357 Magnum, we had no more burglar problems.

In the midst of all that, she had an abandoned nephew to deal with, which, for some, was quite the dilemma, because my biological father was related to Calvin, not Lemell. This wasn't an issue for her. She had taken care of me since I was a toddler. While I appreciated all that Momma had done for me, it wasn't until I met my biological mother's older daughter, Andrea, that I understood how fortunate I was. She was born after I moved in with Calvin and Lemell. I met up with her in 2017 after not seeing her since 1973, and while our reunion was emotional, when the conversation turned to our childhoods, I realized how fortunate I was to have Momma rescue me. Andrea said, "Ray, you were touched by an angel. I wish I had an aunt like Lemell to rescue me out of the hell I grew up in. Boy, you can't begin to imagine how blessed you truly were."

My other sister, Nikia, lived with my biological father for her first three years. He was a violent alcoholic and beat her mother like he did Connie Christmas. Nikia admired Lemell because she was the only woman who stood up to Raymond Sr. She always reminded me how blessed I was to have Lemell Studevent be the one God used to save my life.

Momma was a warrior. My biological mother and father were considerably younger; yet she outlived them by eleven and twenty-one years. She taught us that if we were kind and loving then we would live long. She lived through fifteen presidents and only knew of three.

"JFK loved us," Momma said, "Bill Clinton came close, but Barack was our man. A Black man in the Oval Office, *psst,* I can go see the good LORD now." She said she never thought she'd see the day when we had a brother in the White House.

Momma was my hero. See these chewed up fingernails? That's from me running in the house every time I felt scared, living with my biological mother, who was a heroin addict. Y'all probably thinking, oh, that explains why that fool is so crazy and hyper. I remember one time running from some guys and my friends told me to crawl under a car. I was terrified and claustrophobic. Because when the police used to raid the drug houses in my neighborhood, I hid under the bed or in the closet. See this cut on my lip? I fell down the stairs, but my mother was so drugged up she couldn't help. I nearly bled to death.

You think Lemell–No-Middle-Name–Studevent let me stay in that environment? I was as White as the Klansmen who terrorized her back in the day. You think she would hold that against me and let me stay in that hellhole with my strung-out mother? Come on y'all, this is my Momma we're talking about. A Black woman who grew up in the segregated South chose to raise a rambunctious, White, blue-eyed Negro in the Blackest city in America. I could stand here all day and tell you stories. For the sake of time, I will share some of Momma's favorites.

One day, I left a job application on the table for a Marion Barry summer program. Momma came upstairs and started yelling at me. "Raymond Lorenzo Studevent, are you ashamed of your race? You checked off the box that says you is White. Look here. Look at your birth certificate, it says you a Negro. You ain't White and don't ever forget that!" All I could say was, "Momma, you're the one who said they ain't hiring Black folks. I'm trying to get a job!" Momma struck me with her classic line, "Don't think because you got them blue eyes and that straight hair that you better than us!"

Me and Momma had our private jokes. When people asked how could I be her son, I would say, "If Darth Vader can be Luke Sky-walker's father, why can't she be my momma?" She laughed and told folks I came out of the toaster too early. Needed another scoop of chocolate in the Nestle's mix.

Everybody knew Momma could dress to the nines, but when I was a child, I went shopping with her. She had five different shades for each color. Shoot, Momma had colors that weren't even in the big 120-count Crayola box. Blue, cobalt blue, royal blue, her favorite navy blue, grey, charcoal, ash, pewter. Then there was black! Off black, flat black, onyx, matte black.

I used to get tired of waiting.

"Momma, black is black, so come on, Man."

She'd hit me with, "Boy, black comes in all shades."

I said, "Yeah Momma! Of all people, I know that."

The first time I got a haircut at the neighborhood barber shop, the brother messed up my hair and Momma went back and demanded to know, "Which one of y'all fools messed up my son's hair?" They were stunned that she referred to me as her son. I was proud at that moment. On the way out the door, I stuck my tongue out at the guys in the barbershop.

When *Roots* came out, Black folks, I love y'all but y'all was a little rough on this blue-eyed brother when Kunta Kinté wouldn't change his name to Toby. I watched it, thinking, Boy, it's gonna be rough tomorrow at school. Momma talked to my class to let them know I had a Black mother and that she was not up for any foolishness.

Momma was a prophet. She told me which boys in the neighborhood would turn out to be responsible men and she was right. She taught me to rinse my mouth with peroxide to preserve my teeth and I have never had a cavity. She taught me the importance of reading. In 1977, I was featured in *Ebony Jr.* magazine for reading fifty-one books that summer. Thanks to Momma and that darn curfew, I survived to tell you folks all about it. I can easily name more than twenty guys I know who have been murdered since we were kids.

Momma never missed a day of work Thanks to her example, in more than twenty-five years of work, I never called in sick. Momma taught me to give your best, no matter what.

I appreciated and admired the fact that Momma evolved in her later years. She began to soften up. I teased her that she was trying to get into heaven, so she began to let go of old hang-ups, not easy, but Momma was not a normal old-timer. She came to accept that I became a Jehovah's Witness. "Tell your Jehovah Witnesses friends not to knock on my door too early!"

She always told me if I didn't know the answer to a problem to just pray to the Lord. She taught me to be a father when I had none. I raised my child the best I could, and it turned out great. I learned the importance of treating people kindly and with respect because this world is tough, and sometimes, people just have a bad day.

Momma, while everyone has a legacy, not everyone can be a legend. You are a legend in every sense of the word, Momma. Thank you for rescuing me from a life of poverty and providing me with one full of laughter, fun, and real-life lessons.

You knew it would be hard for me being a Black man inside this White shell. But you prepared me well and I'm so glad that before you left us, you were able to utter the words I longed to hear: "I'm proud of you, Son."

I love you, Momma! You will always be my girl. I'll miss you until the day I take my last breath. You're the greatest momma in the world. May you rest in peace, because you deserve it. There is nothing else to say. Your eighty-eight years of life said it all. We thank you for blessing our lives with the privilege of knowing you. We love you.

EPILOGUE

*"Whenever life presents
you the opportunity to show a
special level of love, always commit
and never walk away."*

S itting on jagged rocks along the Mediterranean Sea in Southern France, I have time to reflect on what's happened since
Momma died a few months ago. After heartfelt prayer, I
decided to delve into my ministry to ease the pain of grieving. I quit
my job and joined Gizelle and my new son-in-law, Seth, on their
missionary journey along the French Riviera, where, as Jehovah's
Witnesses, they preach to African refugees, especially from Nigeria.

During the long flight, I toyed with the idea of writing about my
remarkable life with Momma. I believed it would yield therapeutic
benefits and even bring me the highest level of redemption I could
ever hope to achieve. You see, beyond gaining Momma's approval, I
was still seeking a redemptive sense of peace.

A literary agent I knew gave me her blessing to tell the story.

"A Southern Black woman raising a white, blue-eyed Negro in America's Blackest city? Are you kidding me? What's not to like? Get to work."

Looking along the waterfront, I notice many people reading books and several sitting alone. No one here knows Lemell Studevent, nor do they care. But I do.

Momma always told me that my relentless pursuit of women would be my downfall and keep me from reaching my full potential. Soon after I arrived here, an amazing French woman, named Celine, caught my eye at one of our Kingdom Hall meetings. While the prospect of finding love along the French Riviera sounded much better than digging up old stories and childhood wounds, I couldn't let Momma's prophesy come true, especially at the expense of writing "our" love story.

After dating for nine months, Celine and I mutually ended our romantic relationship, but we have remained close. In fact, just as Momma taught me to help someone in need, I found that opportunity when Celine was diagnosed with breast cancer.

"Whenever life presents you the opportunity to show a special level of love, always commit and never walk away."

Momma's words inspired me to remain in France and take care of Celine through a long and difficult course of treatment. As I close this story, I am in Villefranche-sur-Mer, a famous village on the Riviera. I can see Elton John's house on top of a hill and Bono has a house just a stone's throw away. Not bad for a kid from DC. Of course, this would have never been possible without Momma. Her legacy still guides me, and as I follow her example, I know I can't go wrong.

Afterword

Books have always been about words, and many came to mind in Ray's fascinating memoir.

Belonging.

Ray focuses on the need we all feel to belong, and I felt this yearning throughout his story. It reminded me of a scene from my younger days. Our family had moved away from where I grew up in West Virginia, and every time we visited in our beat-up 1956 black-and-white Chevrolet, it was a true laying on of hands. From far down the road, rolling on bald tires, we passed the Evans' shabby two-story house where all the scraggly grandkids tumbled and played with the chickens in the dirt front yard. Past proud Miss Effie's white, single frame house with the precise black trim and red awning where she first introduced 4-H to our little community. Past the two giant oak trees in the yard where Aunt Rosalee hung her laundry between them to dry. Past ole' pot-bellied Elda Busta, snoozing off another drunken stupor in a lame metal chair leaning against his feeble four-room house.

Jedadiah and Natalie's house still stood where she nursed her peo-
nies in the front yard. Natalie was the only person I ever knew who
looked so White—with blue eyes—that she had to carry an official
card that read: "White Negro."

From our car's road-grimy windows, I could barely make out the
welcome sight of Grandmother, sitting vigil on her front porch. As
soon as the Chevy pulled up and she rose from her chair, I was out
of that car like a shot, dashing through the worn, white-washed gates
past bright yellow daffodils and colorful impatiens flanking my every
step along the dirt path, up the three cement steps to the porch. As
my grandmother's arms drew me in, I laid my head on her heart and
heard her declare my name.

"My baby done come home," she said, which filled my yearning
heart with an immediate sense of belonging.

Fascination and *Intrigue.*

People often tell me, "Oh, your life is so fascinating; you should
write a book about it."

Well, Ray Studevent actually did. His circle of life is full of fascinating intrigue, as "BEN" struggled to learn who he was and how
to be recognized. His story, though, is as much about his amazing
"Momma" as it is about her white-skinned, blue-eyed adopted son.

As a doctoral student at the Ohio State University in the '70s, I
came face to face with trying to find my place in the world. I was
too young to think about legacy, but I knew I wanted to belong, to
make my mark. I had numerous, prestigious opportunities awaiting
me after graduation, none of them really capturing my full desires.
I was awed by the work of Alex Haley in bringing to our culture the
life of activist Malcom X. I had heard that Alex's adventure was to
chronicle the life of his ancestors from sixteenth-century east Africa

to twentieth-century America. Somehow, I felt I was meant to be an integral part of that adventure.

Mystery.

This emerged as Ray tried to get Momma to recognize him when he visited her at an Alzheimer's facility. By this time, he had an adult daughter of his own, and he felt a betrayal of sorts, as though his life may have never existed without Lemell's recognition. That explains his need to recreate their lives together, to cement his legacy and meld their world for eternity.

Transformation.

When I met Alex Haley, his master work, soon to be known as *Roots: The Saga of an American Family,* had been years in the making. I believe the universe brought us together to launch that work into the American conscience. My contribution to birthing it gave me a sense of my own belonging. Although I had my own wonderful mother and precious grandmother (as well as father and siblings), *Roots* allowed me to delve deeply into self-discovery. Through my study of African-American history, I learned facts about Blacks coming from Africa to America. Through *Roots,* I learned the substance of my DNA—what made me who I was and what my potential could be.

Ray's road to transformation was different from that of Malcom and Alex. They grew up as Black men, woven into an America that laid down specific guidelines as to how life was to be lived. For Ray, a dirty blond, blue-eyed Negro, there were few, if any, specific guidelines. There are even fewer today. Black. White. Mixed. African-American. Caucasian. Afro-American.

As Ray related growing from a boy into manhood in the Black community, I chuckled, remembering my passage from a girl into womanhood. The rules. The confusion. What was allowed and what wasn't. What I was supposed to do and what I was prohibited from doing. What was the Black world and what was reserved for Whites. I marveled at how unique life must have been for Ray, being part of neither world, yet straddling both. His skin color. His eye color. His mama's color. His community. His feelings of abandonment, of being lost. Yet in so many ways this was a human struggle, not a racial one. We all search for who we are, where we fit, what we are meant to become.

Wisdom.

In my historical novel *The Treason of Mary Louvestre*, Mary, a slave, learned during the impending upheaval of the Civil War that she did not know who she truly was as she, too, had straddled a Black-and-White world. She came to know what she had to become—not a slave in a White world—but a human being who had a gift to give to make life better, not for herself alone, but for the nation she knew. At great peril to herself, she became an ordinary person who found the courage to perform extraordinary feats of survival that she didn't even know she had the ability to do. Life for her changed when she was transformed, and then found her real place in the world.

Black Sheep is an American story. We all have the blood of many nations flowing through our veins, just as Ray does. His learning to be a man is poignant, yet triumphant. It is interesting and humorous; frightening yet provocative. Very much like the substance of *Roots*, Ray Studevent's story is America, whose story is for us all. Ray and Lemell are our family and our roots. And, in a laying on of hands, we are his!

—*My Haley, PhD*

Acknowledgements

Writing this memoir was more difficult than I thought and more rewarding and surreal than I ever imagined. I could not have pulled this miracle off without the help of the most incredible literary agent imaginable, Leticia Gomez of Savvy Literary Services. She stood by me and walked me through every painstaking chapter. She believed in me and my writing abilities more than I did.

I will be eternally grateful for her incredible generosity and patience, even through tears. Leticia gently pushed me to the limit when she knew my mother had passed. But she was brilliant because she knew that the best would come when my emotions were raw. I love her dearly. She is one-of-a-kind. Her mission is to help authors realize their dreams of having their book published. Leticia has such an altruistic spirit that after a book deal is signed, I believe she is happier than the authors.

Kathy Palokoff, who took time during her vacation and while planning her wedding to put the final editing polish on the book, helped to make sure that the words flowed, and the story jumped off the pages. She is the best.

To My Haley, whose name is synonymous with excellence, who generously wrote the Afterword. My and Alex Haley are literary royalty in the Black community, and I am extremely grateful to have the Haley name associated with this memoir. I recall sitting with Lemell watching *Roots* and remembering the total silence in the room. She would be ecstatic to know that My contributed to our memoir.

A special thanks to my daughter, Gizelle, the sunshine of my life. I am so proud of the incredible woman she has become. It's because of her that I began to turn my life around. May Jehovah continue to bless her efforts. She became my reason for living and believing in life. Her wonderful husband, Seth, served as my IT guy, who patiently helped me fix and figure out all my computer issues during the writing of this book.

I could never have believed in anything without my younger sister, Yolanda "Poochie" Studevent-Coleman. She has given me so much emotional support. She's always been my rock whenever I needed to hear a voice of reason. We have laughed and cried, but we keep on keeping on. Life dealt us a crazy hand, but we are playing it like a Boston in a game of Whist! She told me to tell this story and here it is. I owe much of the motivation to keep fighting life's battles to her. I could easily pen another book on what we've endured and overcome together. She's a true fighter who fought for others far more than she ever fought for herself.

I must thank my oldest sister, Linda, who lived through much of the madness in my young life. She became a social worker after seeing the results of my parents' addictions. She has such a warm heart, and I am so glad that she decided to share it with the world and specifically the children of inner-city DC who, without people like her, wouldn't have a glimmer of hope. Other than Pam Grier, Linda was the coolest Black woman I ever knew in the 1970s.

While many say my story is sad, the story of my sister Cookie is even sadder. When our father died, a tremendous part of her spirit died as well. I want to thank her for showing me what it means to endure and overcome hardship and sadness. Her inner strength helped me persevere through my own trials. Despite watching Momma's fragile body slowly succumb to the merciless onslaught of Alzheimer's, Cookie made Lemell's final years as comfortable as possible. The family will always be grateful for her self-sacrificing spirit.

Nikia Studevent-Hovey, my youngest sister, has gotten more out of her forty-three years than most people do in a lifetime. She dared anyone to tell her she couldn't accomplish something seemingly unattainable. As a shy child, she could barely put two sentences together but has blossomed into an absolute gem, working her way from an English teacher to a school principal. She has always supported me, and for that I am grateful.

My long-lost sister, Andrea "Redds" Caldwell, with whom I reconnected after forty-five years apart, cannot go unmentioned. Sometimes, we forget how incredible someone's presence has been in our life. Redds, along with my cousin Sharon, motivated me to write this memoir. They provided me with a vivid and candid view of what my life could have been like if Lemell had not been the hero she was. Andrea's words, "I wish I would've had a Lemell to rescue me," helped me to appreciate the woman this book celebrates. Despite the difficult hand that life dealt her, Redds overcame it all—a survivor and a "true uptown DC hustler."

My late biological parents, Raymond and Jackie—while certainly irresponsible, they nevertheless gave me one heck of a life. All is forgiven.

Celine, the crazy French gal who stole my heart. At a time when I honestly thought the remaining years of my life would be filled with loneliness, sadness, regret, and despair, she brought me hope and optimism. She taught me that Jehovah, love, and laughter along the French Riviera can heal pain more than any medication. Her faith in Jehovah during her own personal trials has helped me to spiritually mature. *Merci beaucoup.*

After Momma's death, a collection of amazing brothers helped me push ahead and see the importance of relying on Jehovah for the strength I needed to endure. Without their constant loving support, I wouldn't have been able to write this book. More important, they helped me achieve some of my spiritual goals. Thanks to Greg "Sovereignty" Bates, my Dominican "Brother from Another Mother" Edward Perez, Greg "Night Owl" Woodfork, Tony "MacGyver" Campbell, Andre "Banana Bread" Parker, Steve "Do Things Jehovah's Way" McCarthy, Scott "Cool as a Cucumber" Karmazin, Monty "Wildman" McCoullough, Ezra "Level-Headed" Robinson, Joel "Always in a Good Mood" Moody and Lenin "Mi Nica Hermano" Pérez. I am grateful to all these incredible men.

I was once told that Jews and pro bono go together as much as Jews and Arabs. That myth was certainly dispelled by the greatest lawyer in San Diego and probably the world, Alex York. I always heard that you had better get a Jewish lawyer in time of need. Well, my best friend in the world is a Jewish lawyer who helped me in my greatest time of need. He got me six months in a halfway house when I was facing four to six years in a state prison.

His famous words: "I need you to have every person you know to write the judge a letter on your behalf. We want the sentencing date to be on a Friday because judges are usually in a good mood."

They worked! Pro bono! Without Alex, the *Black Sheep* would likely be a dead sheep. Alex has the biggest heart and warmest spirit I've ever known, but he's a pit bull in the courtroom when you need him.

Just a word of acknowledgement to Connie "Brown Sugar" Christmas, whose voice was incredible, but never truly heard. She is the kindest and sweetest woman I have ever known. Whether it's the crackling sound of an old 45 record or as an advocate for the NAACP, her voice is always full of genuine love for the underprivileged and unheard voices across America.

And to Nicaragua's craziest Latina, Geissel "Mi Kardashian bebé de azúcar" Beteta, whose perseverance and determination in overcoming her own trials encouraged me to endure mine. She always made me laugh when I needed it most. *Muchas Gracias!*

HCI BOOKS! They are the best. In the midst of the Covid-19 madness, they kept pushing ahead as if everything was fine. I appreciate their patience and willingness to allow me the creative freedom that every writer dreams of, especially the project overseer, Christine Belleris, and Allison Janse in the public relations department. Yes, "Book Sales Matter!"

To the incomparably gifted editor, David Tabatsky, whose amazing skills shined up *Black Sheep* and made it showroom ready. Thank you.

Finally, to the man behind the machine, Christian Blonshine, thank you for signing off on the project. On behalf of the late Lemell Studevent, I want to thank the entire HCI family for allowing me to be her voice so that the entire world can know how amazing she was.

About the Author

R ay Studevent, Jr. was born in 1967 in Washington, DC, the Blackest city in America, to a White mother who was a heroin addict and a Black father who frequently called prison, "Home Sweet Home."

Ray, nicknamed Ben (Blue-Eyed Negro) by his birth father, had no idea his unique look would take him on a two-sided journey throughout his life. After being abandoned by both parents at the age of five, he was adopted by his aunt by marriage, Lemell Studevent, a beautiful, Black Southern belle, born and raised in the segregated depths of a Southern hell known as Jackson, Mississippi.

While trying to fit into an all-Black neighborhood looking like the all-American boy next door, Ray's greatest challenge was sharing the same roof with an emotionally scarred Black woman who harbored strong resentments toward white-skinned, blue-eyed people. Ray's skin was white as porcelain and his eyes as blue as the ocean, so physically, he represented the epitome of everything Lemell despised.

Lemell had no qualms about repeatedly showing Ray a copy of his birth certificate, which indicated that he was, in fact, of the Black persuasion. Every single day, Ray was forced to fight life on a number of fronts. He had to fight for Lemell's love, fight to survive the mean streets of DC, and most of all fight with the racial identity crisis that constantly haunted him. Every day became a choice to reveal or conceal his racial identity. This struggle made him always take in his surroundings and decide whether it was better to be Black or White in that exact environment.

After seeing several childhood friends murdered and being nearly killed himself, Ray set out to see the world and determine his place within it. After running with Mexican and Black drug dealing gangs in Los Angeles, he landed in prison where he was segregated with racist White inmates. That's when he discovered that Black and White people can be equally racist.

When Ray became overwhelmed with depression from dealing with his identity crisis, he ventured into anything and everything to mask the pain. As he bounced from stand-up comedy, fatherhood, pest control and modeling to become a stock market researcher and eventually a successful businessman, he realized that race plays a critical role in everything he does.

Ray's willingness to partake in so many endeavors has provided him with a fulfilling life. Whether in prison, corporate America, modeling in Lucky Brand jeans or doing stand-up in a smoke-filled comedy club, meeting so many people of various nationalities has given him a perspective as an "undercover brother" that most people can't imagine. By refusing to disclose his race, he has been able to see people's perspectives on different issues, especially the existence of racism at its absolute worst.

Lemell was a librarian who made him read books all summer long and helped him develop an uncanny knack for word play and metaphors. In all his writing, he uses metaphors to convey insightful perspectives on race and race relations, especially those between African-Americans and Whites.

For example, he explores why older Black people hate the movie *King Kong* because of the tribesmen depiction of the stereotypical Black man going crazy for a White woman, and how *Planet of the Apes* depicts a White man falling in love with a Black female ape.

To hear and embrace such things as a white-skinned, blue-eyed African-American child, Ray began his lifelong journey as someone forced to address these issues in a country where the issue of race is so polarizing. He feels that younger generations today have little idea of just how deep the racial divide runs between Black and White communities. In an attempt to raise awareness, Ray uses modern-day illustrations that help others, young and old alike, see race from a simpler perspective.

Ray has aged gracefully, and young people connect with him easily, making him a shoo-in for the college speaking circuit. His nonstop comedic twists and tear-jerking stories create an unforgettable roller coaster ride, full of emotional ups and downs and twists and turns, more than any ride at Disney World can offer.

For more information, or to contact Ray, visit www.raystudevent.com.

This book is dedicated to Lemell Studevent,
and the first copy will be placed at her
tombstone at Arlington National Cemetery,
where John F. Kennedy's eternal flame
burns nearby her gravesite.

While Lemell Studevent was not the
president of the United States, her flame will always
burn bright in the hearts of those
she touched during her eighty-eight years
of life—and none brighter than
inside her baby boy, Ray.

*"May they know that You alone, whose name is Jehovah,
are the Most High over all the earth."*

—PSALM 83:18